■ Please return by the latest date stamped below to avoid a charge.

■ You may renew by telephoning any library in the borough. Please quote the number on the bar code label below.

■ May not be renewed if required by another reader.

BARNE
LONDON BOROUGH

HENDON LIBRARY
ENQUIRIES 020 8359 2628
RENEWALS 020 8359 2629

D0186282

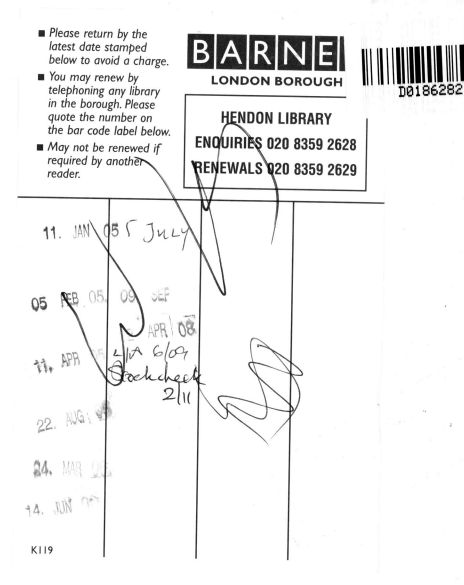

11. JAN 05 ⌐ JULY

05 FEB. 05   09 SEP

APR 08

11. APR   4/1A 6/09
Stockcheck
2/11

22. AUG

24. MAR

14. JUN

K119

30131 03961300 2
LONDON BOROUGH OF BARNET

DYEING AND SCREEN-PRINTING ON TEXTILES

JOANNA KINNERSLY–TAYLOR

A & C BLACK

LONDON

BARNET LIBRARIES	
Cypher	13.08.04
746.6	£24.99

First published in Great Britain 2003
A & C Black Publishers
Alderman House
37 Soho Square
London W1D 3QZ
www.acblack.com

ISBN 0-7136-5180-6

pyright © Joanna Kinnersly-Taylor 2003

A CIP catalogue record for this book is available from the British Library.

Joanna Kinnersly-Taylor has asserted her right under the Copyright, Design and Patents Act, 1988, to be identified as the author of this work.

All rights reserved. No part of this publication may be reproduced in any form or by any means – graphic, electronic or mechanical, including photocopying, recording, taping or information storage and retrieval systems – without the prior permission in writing from the publishers.

Front cover illustration: Joanna Kinnersly-Taylor, detail from one of a series of four wall-hangings, 2001. Photo by Ruth Clark.
Back cover illustrations (from top to bottom): Joanna Kinnersly-Taylor, detail from one of a series of four wall-hangings, 2001. Photo by Ruth Clark.
Michelle House, Untitled (detail), 1999.
Sarah Stephenson, 'Genetics, prompting questions for the future', 2000. Photo by Richard Dawson.
Joanna Kinnersly-Taylor, table linen (detail), 2000. Photo by Ruth Clark.
Frontispiece: Joanna Kinnersly-Taylor (UK) 'Sleepwalker', 2000
Photo by Ruth Clark.

Every effort by the author and publisher has been made to ensure that the information provided in this book is accurate but they can accept no responsibility for any loss, injury or inconvenience sustained by any reader as a result of information or advice contained herein.

Copyright is acknowledged in the text and every effort had been made to contact all copyright holders.

Unless otherwise stated, all photographs, other than artists' work, by Ruth Clark.

Printed and bound in Singapore by Tien Wah Press.

A&C Black uses paper produced with elemental chlorine-free pulp, harvested from managed sustainable forests.

CONTENTS

ACKNOWLEDGEMENTS

I would like to give thanks to Glasgow School of Art and the Department of Printed Textiles for giving me the opportunity to write this book, and to the following staff in particular: Sean Black, Bill Gillham, Mike Graham, Alison Harley, Julie Anne Hughes, Ivor Laycock, Liz Munro, and Alan Shaw and Lindsay Taylor at the Centre for Advanced Textiles. To Ruth Clark, for undertaking the photography so painstakingly; Kim and Vaishali at Double Helix and Timorous Beasties for willingly giving access to their studios, all the textile artists and designers who generously provided images of their work, the suppliers and manufacturers who provided advice and information on their products; to Julia Atkinson, an inspirational tutor; The Surrey Institute of Art & Design, University College, who laid the foundations of my understanding of textile processes and techniques and Sylvia Gordon, for her proofreading and ongoing support. I would also like to thank my husband, Joe Ingleby, for his meticulous illustrations, great patience and understanding.

INTRODUCTION

Sally Greaves-Lord (UK)
'Embrace Hope', solo exhibition at Bankfield Museum, Halifax, 2000
Hand-painted with acid dyes and discharge on silk
Photo: Steve Yates

DYEING AND SCREEN-PRINTING ON TEXTILES is designed to be a user-friendly, informative and inspiring book for the professional textile artist/designer and student alike. It covers many of the key processes used in creating dyed and screen-printed fabrics using a wide range of synthetic dyes for all types of cloth.

With a clear and practical step-by-step approach the reader is guided through every stage of the process from cloth preparation and dyeing, to printing and fixation. Recipes are given for using reactive, direct, vat, acid, disperse and pigment dyes , as well as discharge, devoré, crimping and resist pastes. Heat press processes include transfer printing and application of flock and foil, while the most up-to-date technology – digital printing – is also covered.

The screen-printing process is discussed in detail, and covers areas such as designing and printing a repeat, choosing screens, screen mesh and squeegees, types of stencil and coating, exposing and reclaiming screens. Methods of fixation include instructions on how to make a simple steamer for steaming long lengths of cloth. Advice is also given on equipment needed when setting up a studio.

Alongside this, illustrations of stunning work both by leading textile artists and designers, as well as recent graduates, demonstrate the wide range of textile applications today. This broad spectrum includes large-scale publicly commissioned wall-hangings, one-off gallery pieces, furnishing fabrics and interior accessories, fashion and costume.

I would like to emphasise that as printed textile production is such a vast subject and because there are variations in almost every recipe and process, many down to personal preference and experience, there are not always hard and fast rules. It is with this is mind that I hope the reader will use this book both as a trusted ally in the studio on a day-to-day basis, as well as an inspiring springboard from which to develop further individual exploration.

Joanna Kinnersly-Taylor

CHAPTER ONE

GOOD PRACTICE IN THE STUDIO

The dye mixing bench in the author's studio. Note the three different types of weighing scales. Left to right: basic for weighing larger quantities of ingredients; the economical 'triple beam balance' weighing from 10th of a gram to 2.61kg, and a set of precision scales which weigh from 100th of a gram to 1.5kg.

THE HEALTH AND SAFETY of the textile printer in the studio cannot be stressed enough. For advice on relevant regulatory and legislative requirements, contact the Health and Safety Executive (see address list). They produce an extensive range of publications which provide vital information on, for example, the safe storage, handling and disposal of toxic substances, personal protective equipment including masks, goggles etc. and appropriate fire extinguishers for different types of fires.

Always wear a good quality dust and/or fume mask and rubber gloves when weighing out all dry ingredients, mixing pastes, stirring dye-baths (particularly those exposed to heat), and heat-proof gloves and fume mask when removing cloth from the steamer (especially fabric printed with discharge). Goggles are another essential and these **must** be worn for mixing hazardous chemicals and to protect the eyes from fumes from the steamer (e.g. discharge) or spray from the screen-wash when stripping screens. Open windows as much as possible to ensure good ventilation when carrying out these procedures.

Should you experience any allergic reaction to dyes or chemicals, seek prompt medical advice; be especially vigilant during pregnancy. In case of accidents, have a first aid box, complete with eyewash, to hand. Keep food and drink away from chemicals and the printing area in general.

Keeping the studio clean and tidy ensures high standards of workmanship and efficiency. Wash out utensils and containers immediately after use. Keep work surfaces and scales clean and dry, free of dye or print paste so that work does not get spoiled.

Always use a clean, dry spoon when measuring out dyes to avoid contamination and reseal dye containers properly to maximise life span of the contents. Write the date of purchase on any ingredients and dyestuffs, as some have a short shelf-life. Likewise, always label your mixed pastes with the date they were made.

Store screens safely where they will not get damaged, and either hang squeegees by the handle or store upside down on a shelf, so that the blade does not get distorted. Always wash screens and squeegees immediately after use; pigment can be particularly difficult to remove if left to harden and will block screen mesh.

The print table should be treated with care and cleaned regularly, as a build-up of print pastes, discharge, table gum and masking or parcel tape can spoil the next piece of work, as well as creating an uneven surface. Use hot soapy water and a slightly abrasive cloth or sponge, then wipe over with a clean, damp cloth to remove suds. Pigment should always be wiped off immediately before it hardens. Always take care when ironing down cloth and never pin directly into the table surface.

If possible, have extra electrical sockets positioned where you need them most in your studio to avoid lots of trailing electrical leads when using fan heaters, irons etc.

All old print pastes should be disposed of safely – do not just pour down the sink. Specialist chemical disposal companies will take away toxic waste, but this can be expensive. The best thing is to only mix as much paste as you need. If you do have any small amounts left over, these can be printed off onto newspaper, allowed to dry and then disposed of.

CHAPTER TWO

SETTING UP A STUDIO

The Author's studio within the 'WASPS Factory' – an artists' studio
complex in Glasgow, Scotland
Photo: Keith Hunter

EQUIPMENT AND MACHINERY

WHEN YOU FIRST set up your studio, the list of equipment you need to get started can seem overwhelming. Try not to be too daunted; once you have the basics you can build up other items gradually. If possible, rent the use of expensive equipment, such as an exposure unit, baker or heat press, from your local college or art school. Alternatively, if you are sharing studio space with others, perhaps the cost of a major item can be shared.

Studio layout is very important and it is worth spending some time working this out on paper first. Measure all your equipment and furniture, drawing flat shapes to scale on card and cutting them out. You can then place these on a scale plan (1:20 is a good size), re-arranging items until you have an efficient working space. Position all the water-related equipment in the same area: wash-out, sinks, washing machine etc., with a dye bench nearby. Keep the print table well away from any water, but make sure you have an easy access route to carry screens from the table to the wash-out. The steamer should be near a source of ventilation and a metal cupboard is useful for safe storage of any hazardous or flammable chemicals.

The following outlines the essentials you will need and where you can improvise if on a limited budget.

EXPOSURE UNIT

A professional exposure unit comprises both an ultraviolet (UV) light source and a vacuum frame. In an all-in-one unit, the light source sits underneath thick glass, with the screen positioned horizontally on top. A hinged lid made from rubber is closed down over the screen, and a vacuum pump expels air, sucking the rubber down tightly over the surface of the screen, ensuring excellent contact is made between the screen mesh and the positive. In a vertical unit, once the rubber is holding the screen tightly in place, the frame is tilted through 90° and exposed to UV light housed in a separate unit. The light source may be positioned about 1-2m (3–6.5ft) from the screen, depending on the strength of light, size of vacuum frame and space available.

Exposure unit built by Timorous Beasties for their studio in Glasgow

Most self-employed textile artists/designers do not have their own exposure unit, as they are very costly and can take up a lot of space, requiring a darkroom environment. However, for many of us they are an essential part of the printing process and it is worth finding out if your local art school is willing to rent out this facility. The alternative is to build a simple exposure unit yourself, using either UV or ordinary fluorescent tube lighting inside a shallow box, not more than 30cm (11.5in.) deep. The inside of the unit should be painted white to ensure good reflection of light, with the lighting tubes themselves positioned about 20–25cm (8–10in.) apart and going right to the edges of the box so that the largest screen size possible can be accommodated. The glass top should be made from 10mm ($^3/_8$ in.) safety glass. To ensure that there is good contact between the positive and the screen mesh, foam is placed inside the screen, with a piece of wood the same size positioned on top; heavy weights are then placed on top of this. However, without a vacuum pump, half-tone screens may be difficult to expose using this method. If using fluorescent tubes, the average exposure time may be around 15-20 minutes. The advantage of this light source is that the unit can also be used as a standard light box for painting up positives.

PRINT TABLE

My advice here is to get the biggest you can afford and have space for. A large table allows flexibility in the kind of work you are able to produce. If you are going to be printing repeated lengths, you will need a table at least 3m (10ft) long and, if possible, about 1.55–1.8m (5–6ft) wide (to accommodate furnishing width cloth). When deciding the width of your table, bear in mind that you will need a reasonable amount of space around all sides to access the table easily with (possibly) large screens. The table also doubles up as a valuable space for laying out design work and proposals.

A print table usually consists of a metal framework with large pieces of wood screwed or bolted on top. A 6m (20ft) table may, for example, have 2 x 3m sections, over which an underblanket is stretched. This is then covered with a layer of neoprene, a black synthetic polymer resembling rubber, which is tensioned and secured on the underside of the table, so that no moisture penetrates the blanket. Finally, a metal registration rail runs parallel to the edge of the table. This is the rail where metal 'stops' are positioned in order to register screens for a repeating length. Some tables have adjustable feet, others are bolted to the floor for extra stability. It is possible to make your own table. However, if you are primarily going to be producing repeated lengths of cloth, a more professional table with stop bar is preferable. If well looked after, your print table should last a lifetime.

When getting quotes for tables, check on how much is being charged for carriage and whether the price includes installation. A print table ideally needs to be set up professionally, although in recent years I have had to move mine twice and

TOP At Double Helix's studio in Glasgow, a 10m print table incorporates a 'carriage', allowing large-scale printing to be carried out by one person
ABOVE Printing wallpaper on Timorous Beasties' 20m print table

did manage to re-assemble it satisfactorily. Make sure the table is level and the stop bar parallel to the table, and that the neoprene is sufficiently tensioned to sit smoothly and firmly over the under-blanket. Extremes of temperature can cause incorrectly stretched neoprene to buckle.

WASH-OUT BAY/HOSES

It is essential to have somewhere you can wash out screens quickly and easily, away from your print table. There are various options depending on the type of space you are working in. You can buy lightweight, polypropylene units, which may also be back-lit. They are designed so that the screen sits about 60–80cm from ground level, and you may need to stand on a chair to reach the top of a large screen. Alternatively a tiled floor area with a drain may be more suitable. I have a galvanised steel unit, built to my specifications, so that the screen sits lower down. It also has a 'grill' in the bottom, so that screens can be left to dry off without standing in a pool of water and a rail around the top for an optional

A galvanised steel wash-out bay in the author's studio

shower-type curtain to avoid splashing water in a confined space.

Your screen-wash will obviously need to be situated near a water supply, and ideally you can utilise a tap from your sink(s). Use a trigger-type hose (available from garden centres or DIY stores) for varying water pressure. A power hose (from larger DIY stores) is also needed for cleaning off old screen emulsion at the screen-reclamation stage. This will need to be permanently connected to a water supply (a separate low-level tap can be useful) and will also need to be near a power supply. Bear this in mind when planning your studio.

STEAMER

As outlined in Chapter 12, a home-made dustbin-type steamer is very effective; it is also quite cheap to make. The idea and method of making it came from Suhail Ahmad at the The Surrey Institute of Art & Design, University College, to whom I am very grateful.

You will need an ordinary metal dustbin, 18in. in diameter, and a 'Burco' boiler. Burco is a brand of stainless steel, thermostatically controlled washboilers and catering urns. The Burco should ideally be a minimum 35cm (14in.) in diameter and have a capacity of 26 litres. Turn the dustbin and the Burco boiler upside down and position the Burco centrally on top of the dustbin. Draw around the rim of the Burco onto the bottom of the dustbin and then drill a series of about 84 evenly spaced 6mm ($\frac{1}{4}$in.) holes within this circular area. Then drill four holes at equal intervals into the lid of the dustbin, about 5cm (2in.) from the outside edge. Put a large metal hook

(14cm (5–6in.) long) through each one, securing with a bolt on top, so that about 3cm (1¼in.)is left protruding with the hooks hanging down inside the dustbin. Finally, wrap an insulating jacket (for hot water tanks) around the outside of the dustbin – you may have to cut or fold the jacket to fit. Use gaffer tape to secure the jacket firmly to the top and bottom rim of the dustbin, as well as sticking down any overlapping areas. This jacket helps prevent heat loss during steaming. The dustbin should last a few years (depending on frequency of use) until it needs replacing due to corrosion. The steamer should be plugged directly into a socket (not an extension lead), and the water level checked between steams. Ensure any drips falling from the outside of the steamer are clear of the electrics. Never switch the boiler on without water.

BAKER OR CURER

If you are going to be printing mainly with pigments, a baker will be necessary. As these are expensive, it is worth trying to find second-hand equipment. There are two main styles of baker or curer. The first is a 'wardrobe' type cabinet, often used in art colleges, where the cloth hangs vertically from rails inside. These take up much less space than the larger horizontal type, where the conveyor belt can be set to different speeds and fabric is passed through the machine. This type of baker comes in varying sizes and small, movable machines that plug directly into a normal power supply are suitable for samples and small lengths of cloth. Three-phase electricity will be needed for all larger machines.

Two sizes of infrared conveyor bakers at Double Helix, Glasgow

15

SPIN DRYER/WASHING MACHINE

A spin dryer is essential and a small free-standing one is ideal for samples and small lengths of cloth. However, you will need greater capacity for larger quantities and it is worth considering getting an automatic washing machine or combined washer/dryer. Choose one with a capacity of at least 13kg (28lb); this should accommodate about 10m (32ft) of medium to heavyweight cloth. Always wring out excess water by hand and make sure that the cloth is evenly loaded in the machine. A machine is also very useful for washing backing cloths on a regular basis.

SINK(S)

If space permits, the ideal is to have two sinks: a domestic size sink with a drainer to wash containers and utensils etc. and a larger one for washing out fabric. Catering suppliers are good sources for large, free-standing stainless steel sinks; a double sink is very useful for washing out cloth, as one sink can always be filling up, speeding up the process. Keep the larger sink(s) spotlessly clean so cloth is not marked during washing.

WATER HEATER

A water heater that has a reasonable capacity (at least 15 litres (about 4 US gallons)), is quick to heat up and economical to run is ideal. If you have two sinks, make sure you get a model that is suitable for supplying water to more than one outlet. Thermostatically controlled heaters with a temperature range from about 30–85°C (56–185°F) are suitable. Talk to your local electricity company and plumber for advice on different types of water heater.

SCALES

As discussed in Chapter 3, good record-keeping is essential and you will need to have accurate weighing scales to achieve this. Kitchen scales may be suitable for weighing larger quantities of ingredients, but are not accurate enough for small amounts of dyestuff or cloth (see also Chapter 5). Electronic precision scales, however, are very expensive, so it is worth trying to find second-hand or reconditioned scales from suppliers or university laboratories. A 'triple beam balance' is a much more affordable manual alternative, available calibrated to a hundredth of a gram, although not quite as easy to use. A tare facility is also useful as it enables several ingredients to be weighed consecutively into the same container.

DYE BENCH/TABLE

It is preferable to have a separate area for weighing out and mixing dyes and pastes, positioned near the sink. Have two sockets positioned at this point, for scales and an electric mixer. A domestic hand mixer is invaluable for ensuring pastes are mixed thoroughly; if you need to mix up large quantities of gums on a regular basis, a catering or industrial mixer may be beneficial. Make sure your scales sit on a firm surface, as they are very sensitive. Shelves above are useful for storing all your ingredients.

◄ Joanna Kinnersly-Taylor (UK)
'The Transparent Architecture of Jellies', 1999
Dyed and screen-printed with reactive dyes and discharge on linen – 180cm x 500cm
Photo: Ruth Clark

SCREENS

Overall, I would recommend aluminium framed screens rather than wooden ones. Although they are more expensive, they don't warp, are quicker to dry and are also lighter and therefore more manageable on a large scale, especially if printing alone. You may have different screen requirements depending on whether you are doing repeat lengths or one-off placement prints.

If you are going to be using a registration rail, check your screen frame is at least the same depth as the distance between the table surface and the top of the rail in order for brackets or clamps to work against stops set against the rail. A fairly standard frame depth is 4cm (1½ in.).

Screens will also need to have a means of fixing on brackets – see also Chapter 11, 'Attaching the bracket to the screen'. Wooden screen frames have the advantage here as a bracket made from steel flat bar can simply be drilled and screwed straight into the frame, providing the wood is soft enough. Aluminium frames will need to either incorporate some means of allowing a bracket to be screwed in, or clamps can be used. If you do choose wooden screens, make sure they are made from a reasonably water-resistant timber that is not too heavy. The corners should be screwed and glued to provide long-term resistance against the constant wet/dry conditions.

If you have enough storage space, it can be useful to have quite a lot of (different sized) screens, because it takes the pressure off having to clean off images you may wish to go back to at a later date, and also the probable inconvenience and expense of re-exposing. Ideally, screens should be stored in a screen rack where they will be protected from damage; if not, stack vertically in a corner in order of size so that no screen leans onto the mesh of another. Ensure there is enough room to pull out, lift and turn the largest screen, without knocking into any other piece of equipment or furniture – it's very easy to rip screen mesh.

NOTE:

- It can be useful to number your screens and keep a corresponding list noting the mesh size, overall frame and corresponding maximum image sizes, together with what imagery is on the screen

Screen mesh

Traditionally, screen mesh was made of silk, but nowadays polyester provides a much more durable and economical alternative. This polyester 'silk' is available as two main types: multifilament and monofilament. Mostly it is available as a plain weave, and occasionally as a twill.

MULTIFILAMENT This mesh is the cheaper of the two, each strand being made of several strands twisted together. This creates a somewhat rougher surface, and after time a residue of emulsion (if used) and/or pigment can build up around the design area, making the screen much harder to strip. Generally, use of multifilament mesh would be confined to working with paper stencils or using resist techniques with pastes, litho or wax crayons etc. painted or drawn directly onto the screen. Multifilament mesh size denotes the size of the opening between the threads and is described with a number followed by an 'XX'; the smaller the number, the larger the opening and the coarser the mesh. This mesh comes in sizes ranging from 6XX (very coarse) to about 16XX (very fine). For textile printing purposes, a 10XX, 12XX, or 14XX would be suitable.

MONOFILAMENT This describes a mesh woven from single strands of fibre, which can be made into much finer mesh than can be achieved with multifilament. This is the mesh I would recommend using as it will last a long time, withstanding endless stripping and re-coating, and also provide a suitable surface for transferral of artwork produced by almost all methods. Monofilament mesh size is indicated by a number which denotes the number of threads per linear centimetre or inch, followed by 'T'. The smaller the number, the coarser the mesh. It depends on the type of work you will be carrying out as to which mesh size you choose. A 62T (160T) mesh size is ideal for general use and with half-tones; 55T (140T) or 49T (125T) are also fairly multi-purpose. 90T is suitable for *very* fine imagery, especially small text, but will block easily with pigments. If you are printing onto a coarsely woven cloth with a bold image, especially in pigments, a slightly larger mesh (43T) may be appropriate. For large flat areas of metallic pigment, an even coarser mesh, say 38T (95T), may be necessary to prevent drying out and blocking. It is important to remember that the coarser the mesh, the more difficult it is to print smooth curves, as these will appear 'stepped'.

SQUEEGEES

It is worth getting the best quality squeegees that you can afford; if looked after properly, these will provide you with many years of service. Your selection of squeegee sizes will relate to the internal widths of your screens. The squeegee should fit comfortably within the screen (allowing a few centimetres at each side), so that it does not scrape against the frame when printing. It is best to get the largest squeegee appropriate for each different frame, so that it can be utilised for printing the maximum range of image sizes, ideally allowing 3cm (1 ¼ in.) beyond each edge of the image. A very small squeegee of about 16cm (6 ¼ in.) is useful for printing colour samples.

There are a variety of different blade types and finishes and with either wooden or metal handles. Choice is down to personal preference and the type of work being undertaken. Squeegee blades are made of natural or synthetic rubber (neoprene) or polyurethane. The former types wear slightly more quickly but create minimal electrostatic charge, whereas polyurethane has greater resistance to abrasion but becomes more highly charged with static; both materials harden with age. Squeegees can be shaped to a range of different profiles, from square and V-shaped, through varying degrees of roundness to 'mushroom' shaped blades. Generally speaking, a sharper blade requires less ink, with a reduction in opacity of print. Most textile printers prefer to use a

MESH SIZE CONVERSION

monofilament threads per cm	monofilament threads per inch	multifilament size of opening
34T	86T	6XX–7XX
38T	95T	8XX
43T	110T	10XX
49T	125T	12XX
55T	140T	12XX
62T	160T	14XX
70T	180T	14XX
78T	200T	16XX
92T	232T	16XX
96T	245T	16XX

square or slightly rounded V-shaped profile squeegee of medium hardness (see below) as it allows for a range of printing situations; an overly rounded blade can deposit too much ink on the fabric and will cause a fine image to flood, resulting in loss of detail. Remember that a new squeegee will take a little time to break in and may 'judder' across the screen mesh at first, especially if printing a large image.

There is a choice of blade hardness and this is expressed in 'degrees shore', denoted by a number ranging from about 60 (soft) to 95 (very hard), with most squeegees made to 65, 75, or 85 degrees shore. A softer squeegee is more suited to printing solid overall patterns on substrates with an uneven surface, whereas a medium blade (70–75) is better for large formats and half-tone printing. The flexibility of the print table surface should be taken into account when choosing a blade; a softer surface would require a harder blade and vice versa. Depending on frequency of use, the squeegee blade will eventually wear, and some suppliers offer a blade sharpening service. When purchasing new squeegees, ensure that the screws or bolts which clamp the wooden or metal handle around the blade actually *go through* the blade itself. If not, the blade can work loose after a relatively short time (especially if the squeegee has a wooden handle) and the squeegee will be useless. Never leave squeegees soaking in water to clean, or store blade side down, as they will warp.

COATING TROUGHS

A coating trough is used to apply photographic emulsion to the screen. It is a relatively expensive item, but absolutely essential for successful screen exposure, as it is the best implement to

Coating trough; normally made from brushed aluminium with removable plastic ends.

give an even coating of the emulsion at the correct thickness. Troughs are normally made from brushed aluminium and have detachable plastic ends. You should choose sizes that relate to your main screen sizes, allowing for a gap of about 1–1.5cm ($^1/_2$–$^3/_4$ in.) at each end between trough and edge of screen frame to give a bit of 'spring' and tension for even coating. If your emulsion system requires coating the mesh on the *inside* of the screen as well as the outside, remember to take this into account when choosing the trough size. Two or three sizes of trough are normally adequate for a range of screen sizes. The first should relate to your smallest screen and then this can be used either alone, or in conjunction with a bigger trough, to coat larger screens in sections. Always clean the trough and plastic ends thoroughly and immediately after use, as it is vital the edge of the trough does not get clogged with hardened emulsion, otherwise it will not be possible to apply the coating evenly.

Patricia Black (Australia)　▶
'Cocoon', 1999; commissioned for a performance by the Costume and Textile Museum, Venice
Bound shibori processes with discharge; twisted and tied points applied over the whole cloth using cotton twine ('kumo')

DYES AND AUXILIARIES

As dyes are very expensive and some have a limited shelf life, it is best to try and order relatively small quantities. As with most things however, it is obviously cheaper buying in bulk, so it might be worth sharing a dye order with a colleague. The same goes for all the other ingredients needed to make pastes, discharge, gums etc. It is a question of finding the balance between cost and the convenience of not running out of ingredients at a crucial time when you are working towards a deadline. All ingredients *must* be kept in airtight containers, away from direct sunlight or excessive heat. Always label ingredients with the date of purchase and never label anything on the lid, as it is easy to replace the wrong one on the wrong container! See 'The Colour Index' in Chapter 5, for information on dye identification.

CONTAINERS

There are various sizes and types of containers that will be invaluable in your studio. These are as follows:

- Pyrex measuring jug – for checking colour of water when rinsing out cloth and general measuring of liquid
- Stainless steel jugs, 0.5l and 1l (1 and 2 US pints) – have a narrow base which is ideal for dissolving small quantities of dyestuff; can be heated
- 'Tri-Pour' beakers, from laboratory suppliers, in 0.5l, 1l, 2l (1, 2 and 4 US pints) – ideal for mixing and storing print pastes and discharge etc. The triangular rim is perfect for scraping excess paste off the screen and clingfilm can

easily be held in place with an elastic band, for keeping fresh
- Plastic tubs with lids, 2l (4 US pints) or larger – for mixing up and storing thickeners
- Plastic and stainless steel (if using heat source) buckets, 10l (2½ US gallons), with volume marked in 1l increments

SMALL STOVE

An electric two-ring tabletop stove is very useful for heating and dissolving ingredients in a stainless steel jug.

FAN HEATERS

These are very useful for speeding up drying of screens, cloth and print table after washing and/or gumming. Remember not to dry printed cloth too harshly, especially with certain processes; also when drying screens, position heaters *at least 60cm (24in.)* from the mesh otherwise it can melt.

BACKING CLOTHS

Backing cloths can be made from a variety of fabrics, depending on the user's requirements. They are for use both on the print table as a cloth in which to pin your fabric or as a means of wrapping work for steaming. Where backing cloths are described for processes in this book, these are made from cotton 'duck'. The term originates from the Dutch word *doek* meaning a linen canvas used for sailors' garments, although nowadays, duck is used to describe a broad range of fabrics. Duck is normally a very tightly woven cotton, in a plain weave using double warp and double weft threads, making it strong, durable

Jason Pollen (USA)
'Dharma Light', 1997
Fused silk, reactive dyes, painted, printed, vat dye discharge – 81cm x 140cm
Photo: Matthew McFarland, Kansas City

and particularly suitable for use as backing cloth material. Cotton duck comes in various weights and it is usually necessary to have something between 7½–10oz. Anything lighter will not be able to withstand drips from the steamer, or be substantial enough to pin into, whereas a cloth that is too heavy will not allow adequate steam penetration. Choose a width that suits your table but remember when you first wash the cloth, it will shrink quite a lot. A 150cm (59in.) wide cotton duck will reduce to about 138cm (54in.) in width and approximately 10–12cm (4–5in.) per metre in length. A final width of 138cm (54in.) suits a table 150cm (59in.) wide and is also ideal for the dustbin and Burco steaming method described.

SUNDRIES

- Mask (dust and fume), goggles, gloves (rubber and heat-proof)
- Syringes, pipettes and measuring cylinders
- Spoons, spatulas, ladles, sieve
- Thermometer (a jam making thermometer is suitable and easily available)
- Hydrometer with Baumé or Twaddell scale (if required
- Funnel
- Newsprint
- Tailor's chalk
- Pins
- Masking tape
- Gummed tape/parcel tape
- Steel metre rule and right angle
- Kilt pins for suspending cloth inside the steamer
- Extension lead(s)
- Steam iron
- Pinking shears

PREMISES, FUNDING, SETTING UP AND RUNNING YOUR BUSINESS

For the most comprehensive advice on all these aspects, I recommend the Crafts Council's excellent *Running a Workshop; Basic Business for Craftspeople* (see Bibliography for details). The book covers everything from grants and funding, finance and administration, costing and pricing, to selling, promotion and publicity, and exhibiting. It includes the addresses of the Regional Arts Boards and Arts Councils in the UK, as well as other funding and advisory bodies and commissioning agencies.

Another valuable source of information is on [a-n] The Artist Information Company web site at www.anweb.co.uk. This site has over 1,000 pages covering artists' practice, business, visual arts careers and artists' stories. [a-n] also publish a range of visual arts contracts and monthly [a-n] magazine, which is the main notice-board for commissioning opportunities. See the address list for further details.

CHAPTER THREE

RECORD-KEEPING

The author's dye notebook, record books and samples

I BELIEVE THIS is an important aspect of working practice. Some may see it as a laborious procedure that reduces spontaneity, but I think it can be made to work as a powerful tool, enhancing your skills and rather than restrict creativity, actually bring it into focus.

An enormous amount of time, energy and preparation goes into producing any printed cloth, yet the actual physical action of screen-printing can take just a few seconds. To arrive at the point where one produces a successful print may have taken days of sampling – trying out different fabrics, colours, techniques etc. – and it is this process of sampling and accurate record-taking that will pay off in the end result.

Each time you produce a range of samples, you are adding to a valuable store of information, which gradually builds up and provides a unique reference source for every new project you carry out.

When you undertake a commission or project, time-scale is often very tight. You may not have time (or money) to make mistakes and you need to know you can get the job done efficiently and professionally. Therefore, I cannot stress enough how worthwhile it is to make all your mistakes at the sample stage and be aware of why things do or do not work, so that you can proceed to the final work with confidence.

The keys to record-keeping are accurate measuring and consistency of process, ensuring that when a technical problem occurs it can be pinpointed and eliminated. Without this, your dye-notes will be useless.

Everyone develops their own method of record-keeping that works for them. The main thing is to keep it clear and simple and record things in a way that you will understand when you go back to them six months later. The following notes describe the basics of how I keep my own technical records and these can be adapted to suit your own requirements.

I always use a 'dye notebook'; this is basically just a diary of every technical process I carry out in my studio, from dyeing cloth and mixing colours to noting down how much a certain fabric shrinks or the order of printing. This may sound laborious, but it saves an enormous amount of time and worry in the future.

All colour samples, whether dyed, printed, dis-charged, devoré etc., end up mounted onto A6 size cards with a strip of double-sided tape at the top. This seems to be a practical solution, as the cards fit into 6 x 4in photo storage sheets which give protection from splashes and spills, and the samples are big enough to lay against other colours/fabrics etc. – a very small swatch can be difficult to use. On the reverse of each card I record all the relevant information: recipe, number of pulls, method of fixation (and temperature, if relevant), type of cloth and supplier, date, page number in notebook to which it refers and job/project title. The sheets can then be stored in ring binders.

Although specific recipes are given later in the book, here are a few tips that ensure your dye notebook and record-keeping works for you.

DYEING SAMPLES

It is important when dyeing samples that you use a reasonable sized piece of cloth. A very small square of fabric dyed in a jug, for example, will not be accurate enough. If possible, use a piece of cloth at least 16 x 40cm (6 x 15in.).

Write out the full recipe/calculation in your dye notebook before starting and have it to hand near your scales so there is no danger of mis-weighing ingredients. Remember to pay special attention to the water quantity, as this will be crucial if you repeat the recipe, particularly with a larger piece of cloth. (See 'Liquor ratios for different dyeing situations' in Chapter 5).

After dyeing, cut a swatch from your cloth and stick it on the relevant page below the recipe.

Then cut a larger piece to mount onto an A6 size card and record the recipe on the reverse as described above.

PRINT PASTES

In mixing and testing print pastes, I brush on a sample of colour in my notebook by the appropriate recipe; this makes it much easier to locate information later on. For print paste samples, I screen print 6cm (2¼ in.) squares of colour, which fit the A6 size sample card.

DISCHARGE

It is useful to build up a record of the dischargeability of both dyed backgrounds and as overprints on different strengths of print pastes. Again I will print 6cm (2¼ in.) squares of discharge onto a dyed cloth, or two different strength discharges overprinted down each side of a 6cm (2¼ in.) colour square in 2cm (¾ in.) strips. By working in this way, a surprising range of colours can be achieved on a piece of dyed cloth by printing and overprinting in *different orders* using just one print paste colour and one or two different strengths of discharge.

It is worth noting that colour/discharge samples printed in this way (flat colour) at this size (6cm (2¼ in.) squares with 2cm (¾ in.) strips) represent the *optimum* result achievable on that particular cloth. Because the printed area is small, pressure applied by the squeegee will be disproportionately greater to any larger sized print.

Wendy Edmonds (UK)
Scarves - filigree, twist, grid
Heat transfer print with disperse dye on microfibre, polyester chiffon and crêpe
Photo: Nick Turner

Therefore, a bigger or more detailed image may require more pulls or a longer steaming time to create the same effect.

CHAPTER FOUR

SELECTING AND PREPARING CLOTH

Squigee (UK)
Puff printed cotton velvet curtains; puff, and puff and pigment printed linen mix cushions
Photo: Matte Gibb

WHEN YOU choose cloth for dyeing and printing, the main concern will be its suitability for the end product or use. There will be all kinds of practical and aesthetic considerations and success will depend on matching the right cloth with the appropriate dyes, print pastes and techniques.

Whether you are making site-specific textiles to commission, or your printed cloth is for garments, accessories or furnishings, some or all of the following will have to be taken into account: durability, method of cleaning and wash and lightfastness, flameproofing and, for wall hung work, means of finishing and fixing.

FIBRE TYPES

Fibres can be classified into two groups: natural fibres and man-made fibres. Within each group are two main categories of fibre:

NATURAL FIBRES

Cellulose (derived from plants): includes cotton, linen (flax), jute, sisal, ramie, hemp, pineapple.

Protein (derived from animals): includes wool, mohair, alpaca (South American camel, llama family), llama, cashmere (Tibetan or Kashmir goat), angora (rabbit), silk – Bombyx (white, cultivated silkworm), silk – tussah (cream/brown, wild silkworm).

MAN–MADE FIBRES

Regenerated fibres (made from wood cellulose): includes viscose rayon, cellulose acetate, cellulose triacetate, Modal, rubber.

Synthetics (made from chemical substances called polymers): includes nylon (polyamide), polyester, acrylic, elastane, polypropylene.

IDENTIFYING FIBRES

A simple way of identifying fibres is to carry out a burn test.

Fibre	Burns or melts	Type of flame	Rate of burning/ melting	Smoke colour	Smell	Residue
Natural: Cellulose						
Cotton	burns	yellow	fast	grey	burnt paper	fine, soft, grey ash
Linen	burns	yellow	fast	grey	burnt paper	smouldering soft grey ash
Natural: Protein						
Wool	burns	irregular, slight hiss	slow	blue/ grey	burnt hair or feathers	crisp, black bead, crushes easily
Silk	burns	irregular, slight hiss	slow	grey	burnt hair or feathers	crisp, black bead, crushes easily
Man-made: Regenerated Fibres						
Viscose rayon	burns	yellow	fast	grey	burnt paper	fine, soft, grey ash
Cellulose acetate	melts	yellow	fairly slow	grey	burnt paper, vinegar	scorched bead, crushes
Cellulose triacetate	melts	yellow	fairly slow	grey	burnt paper, vinegar	scorched bead, crushes

Fibre	Burns or melts	Type of flame	Rate of burning/ melting	Smoke colour	Smell	Residue
Man-made: Synthetics						
Nylon	melts	yellow	quite fast	grey	celery	very hard, light brown bead
Polyester	melts	yellow	quite fast	grey	quite sweet	very hard, black bead
Acrylic	melts	luminous	very fast	black	acrid	hard, black irregular bead

PREPARATION OF CLOTH PRIOR TO DYEING AND PRINTING

Many fabrics will already be prepared for dyeing and printing, (often referred to by suppliers as 'PFD') having undergone a process of de-sizing, scouring, bleaching and mercerisation (cotton), although you may wish to put them through the washing machine first anyway. However, in some cases, the cloth may be stiff or smell waxy, as a result of natural or added fats and waxes applied during weaving, together with impurities such as size and starch. These now need to be removed in order for the fibres to react with dyes and pastes effectively and evenly. Cloth may also be in a 'grey' or 'loom-state' condition, appearing beige in colour, and you may wish to bleach the cloth after scouring, for maximum colour accuracy (particularly if you are dyeing a pale shade). If you are uncertain whether a cloth needs scouring, place a small piece on the surface of a jug of water. If it wets out easily and sinks rapidly to the bottom, it will probably have been scoured; if it floats and does not absorb the water, it will need cleaning. If you are uncertain, always test dye a small piece first. Avoid fabrics with a permanent-press or Scotchgard finish as these are extremely difficult and hazardous to remove. During the scouring or bleaching process, always allow enough water for cloth to move freely. When cloth preparation is complete, remember to dry fabric before the dyeing process, to allow accurate weighing and dye calculation.

NOTE:

- All the following recipes use 'Metapex 26', which is a trade name for a 'pH-neutral' detergent, widely used in cloth preparation and finishing. However, any domestic brand that states 'pH-neutral' on the bottle, will be suitable

SCOURING

COTTON AND LIGHTWEIGHT LINEN

1 Boil in a solution of 10g sodium carbonate per litre water and 2ml Metapex 26 per litre water for 30 minutes.

2 Rinse thoroughly in warm water, spin and dry.

NOTE:

• Sometimes linen will be in a 'half-bleached' state and this refers to the amount of natural colour retained and is not due to inadequate scouring. This natural shade may need to be taken into account if dyeing a pale colour; alternatively, bleaching may lighten the colour further

HEAVYWEIGHT LINEN

A heavyweight linen, especially one that is still 'grey' or in 'loom-state', may need a slightly different treatment, which combines scouring, de-sizing and bleaching.

1 Prepare a bath at 40°C (104°F) and add 1g sodium silicate, 1g sodium peroxide, 1g sodium bicarbonate and 1ml Metapex 26 *all* per litre water. Add the linen, keeping the cloth as open as possible, and over a period of 45 minutes gradually raise the temperature of the bath to 85°C (185°F).

2 Rinse well in warm water, spin and dry.

WOOL

1 Prepare a bath at 40°C (104°F) and add Metapex 26 at 1% of the dry weight of the wool.

2 Gently push the wool under the water and move occasionally over the next 30 minutes –

do not handle excessively otherwise felting will occur.

3 Rinse gently in warm water, spin and dry.

NOTE:

• If scouring wool in fleece form, place in a pillowcase or similar to spin dry. Afterwards, separate fibres gently and either dye immediately or dry in a well-ventilated place, away from direct heat and sunlight; do not tumble dry

SILK

Silk is normally 'de-gummed', ie. the natural gum sericin and other machine oils have been removed, but raw silks like tussah may need to be treated.

1 Prepare a bath at 85°C (203°F) with 3g soap flakes per litre water and treat the fabric for 45–90 minutes. Do not boil.

2 Rinse well first in warm and then cold water, spin and dry.

VISCOSE RAYON, CELLULOSE TRIACETATE, NYLON, POLYESTER

1 Prepare a bath at 70°C (158°F) with 15ml Metapex 26 per litre water and 20g sodim carbonate per litre water and treat the cloth for 30 minutes.

2 Rinse well in cold water, spin and dry.

CELLULOSE ACETATE AND ACRYLIC

1 Wash in a bath containing 15ml Metapex 26 per litre water at 60°C (140°F) for 30 minutes and rinse well in warm water. Spin and dry.

BLEACHING

For best results, cloth should always be scoured prior to bleaching.

COTTON AND LINEN

Cellulose fibres require an alkali bleaching bath.

1 Make up a bath with cold water and add 10ml sodium hypochlorite at 4% strength (ordinary household bleach) per litre water, together with 5g sodium carbonate per litre water.
2 Enter the cloth into the bath and leave until the desired whiteness is achieved; this may take from 1–4 hours, or sometimes may need to be left overnight. *Do not heat the bleaching bath.*
3 Rinse cloth thoroughly, and neutralise any alkali remaining in the fibres by subsequently rinsing in a bath containing 1ml acetic acid (20%) per litre water.
4 Rinse again, spin and dry.

NOTES:

- Do not exceed bleach quantities, as fibres can be damaged and cloth weakened
- If a really intense white is required, the cloth can be further treated with an optical brightening agent (OBA). OBA's do not remove colour from the fabric, like a bleach, but instead add themselves to the fabric, like a colourless dye. After treatment, the cloth absorbs ultraviolet light and converts it into visible white light, giving the fabric an enhanced bright whiteness

1 Make a bath at 40°C (104°F) containing a suitable OBA measured at 0.5% on dry weight of cloth. Stir gently for 5–10 minutes.
2 Rinse thoroughly in cold water, spin and dry.

WOOL AND SILK

Protein fibres require an acid bleaching bath, however, tussah silk (cream/brown) cannot be bleached.

1 Make a bath at 50°C (122°F). Add hydrogen peroxide (dilution as in List of Auxiliaries) in the following proportion: 1 part hydrogen peroxide (30 volume) to 15 parts water, ie. 1 litre to every 15 litres water.
2 Add 2g sodium silicate per litre water and stir carefully to dissolve. Sodium silicate gives the bath the slight alkalinity required, controlling the oxidizing action and increasing bleaching efficiency of the chemicals on the cloth.
3 Enter *pre-wetted* cloth, gently submerge under the water and leave for up to 6 hours or overnight if necessary. *Do not heat the bleaching bath.*
4 Rinse thoroughly, spin gently and dry.

If further whitening is required:

1 Make a bath at 50°C (122°F) containing a suitable OBA for protein fibres measured at 0.5–1.5% on dry weight of cloth, together with 1.5g sodium hydrogen sulphite per litre water. Treat for up to 1 hour.
2 Rinse thoroughly in cold water, spin and dry.

SUMMARY OF SCOURING RECIPES

Fabric	Temperature	Auxiliaries	Scouring time	Rinsing / Finishing
cotton and lightweight linen	100°C (212°F)	sodium carbonate Metapex 26	30 minutes	thoroughly in warm water / spin & dry
heavyweight linen	40°C (104°F) > 85°C (185°F)	sodium silicate sodium peroxide sodium bicarbonate Metapex 26	45 minutes	thoroughly in warm water / spin & dry
wool	40°C (104°F)	Metapex 26	30 minutes	gently in warm water / spin gently & dry away from direct heat and sunlight (if in fleece form)
silk – tussah (cream/brown)	85°C (203°F)	soap flakes	45–90 minutes	warm then cold water / spin & dry
viscose rayon, cellulose triacetate, nylon, polyester	70°C (158°F)	Metapex 26 sodium carbonate	30 minutes	thoroughly in cold water / spin & dry
cellulose acetate, acrylic	60°C (140°F)	Metapex 26	30 minutes	thoroughly in warm water / spin & dry
nylon	70°C (160°F)	Metapex 26 sodium carbonate	a few minutes	thoroughly in cold water / gently spin & dry

SUMMARY OF BLEACHING RECIPES

Fabric	Temperature	Auxiliaries	Scouring time	Rinsing / Finishing
cotton and linen	cold do not heat the bleaching bath	sodium hypochlorite (4%), sodium carbonate	1–4 hours or overnight	thoroughly in cold water / neutralise any alkali remaining by subsequently rinsing in 1ml acetic acid (20%) per litre water / spin & dry
may be further treated with an optical brightening agent (OBA)	40°C (104°F)	suitable OBA at 0.5% on weight of cloth	5–10 minutes	thoroughly in cold water / spin & dry
wool and silk	50°C (122°F) do not heat the bleaching bath	hydrogen peroxide, sodium silicate	up to 6 hours or overnight	thoroughly in cold water / spin gently & dry
may be further treated with an optical brightening agent (OBA)	50°C (122°F)	suitable OBA at 0.5–1.5% on weight of cloth, sodium hydrosulphite	1 hour	thoroughly in cold water / spin gently & dry

CHAPTER FIVE

DYEING CLOTH

Please also refer to the 'Dyeing samples' notes in Chapter 3.

Selection of suitable vessels for dyeing samples and smaller pieces of cloth.

TYPES OF VESSEL

Any vessel made from a material that is resistant to chemicals and easy to clean will be suitable for cold water dyeing; glass, enamelled or galvanised metal, and plastic (polythene) bowls, buckets or baths are all appropriate. For dyeing recipes that require the dye-bath to be heated, stainless steel is the best option. *Never* expose galvanised metal to direct heat, as it will give off toxic zinc fumes.

WATER

Generally, water used in all dyeing and printing processes should be soft water. If you live in a hard water area, you should add a water softener such as 'Calgon', following manufacturer's instructions.

LIQUOR RATIO

This is the relationship between the weight of cloth and quantity of water required in the dye-bath. There is varying opinion on liquor ratios, but to ensure even dyeing, it is important to have enough water to be able to easily move the cloth around in the dye-bath, whilst not using an excessive amount, which can prevent dye from reaching the fibres. Either extreme can be a factor in uneven dyeing. Each type of dye requires a slightly different liquor ratio and this is given with each recipe. If you do experiment with alternative ratios, it is important to be consistent in your choice within each group, in order to build up coherent records. If the liquor ratio is 20:1, this is worked out as 20 x weight of cloth = amount of water required (in ml). As 1ml of water weighs 1g, this makes the calculation very simple. For example, 20 x cloth weighing 150g = 300ml water. Remember that the liquor required is the *total* volume of water in the dye-bath, and this should be taken into account when wetting out cloth and dissolving dyestuff.

LIQUOR RATIOS FOR DIFFERENT DYEING SITUATIONS

Final water quantity will also depend on the size and shape of vessel and how bulky the cloth is. This can particularly be the case when using a winch dyer, where it is essential to cover the heating elements, and allow enough water for the large quantity of cloth to be rotated easily through the dye-bath. It therefore may be necessary to increase the amount of water by doubling, or even tripling it; i.e. 20 x weight of cloth x 2 or 3. Remember the rule of not having unnecessarily large amounts of water. However, if you do increase the water quantity, you must increase the amounts of any other ingredients which relate directly to it. The amount of dyestuff is always measured in relation to the weight of cloth, so this never changes.

As it is very important to replicate dyeing conditions from your sample dyeing to dyeing of actual length, you should use the same liquor ratio for each. I recommend *first* working out how much water the large piece of cloth will require. For example, if you are dyeing a 12m length of habotai silk in a winch dyer, despite the volume of cloth, the weight will be low and result in a quantity of water that probably will not be adequate. Therefore, if you need to triple the water quantity, then *triple* the water quantity at the *sample dyeing stage* also:

weight of habotai silk = 15g x 20 = 300ml water x 3 = 900ml water.

Remember to always note down the final water quantity and liquor ratio, and the type of vessel used for dyeing in your dye notes.

THE COLOUR INDEX

The Colour Index is a comprehensive list of all known dyestuffs and includes data on use and means of application, fastness properties, dischargeability, trade names, chemical structure, inventor and patent. It also incorporates a list of dye and pigment manufacturers. The nine volume Index is updated quarterly and is now available on CD-ROM from the Society of Dyers and Colourists.

It is helpful to understand the system of naming dyes, especially if a colour chart is not available when purchasing. Each dye group has a different trade name depending on the manufacturer; for example, two brands of reactive dye are Procion and Cibacron. The same Colour Index number is given to dyes of the same type and colour, so that providing the relevant number is known, the correct equivalent can be located anywhere in the world. The letters following the dye colour are derived from the German words for the three primary colours: **Rot** (red), **Gelb** (yellow) and **Blau** (blue), and these indicate the shade. For example, Rubine MX-B, denotes a slight leaning towards blue. If a number prefixes the letter, this tells you how much of that particular primary colour exists in the dye and this is measured on a scale of 1–10, with 10 being the greatest amount. Therefore, in Red MX-8B there is a strong presence of blue and in Blue MX-2G, a small amount of yellow. In the case of yellow, a suffix of 'G' relates to 'grün' (the German word for green), so Yellow SP-8G indicates a yellow with a large quantity of green added.

FASTNESS PROPERTIES OF DYES

Details of fastness properties of dye-stuffs is included with other key information in manufacturers' dye pattern books. Ratings are based on results of globally agreed tests of fastness. Washfastness is measured on a scale of 1–5 with 5 being very fast. Fastness to light is expressed on a scale of 1–8, with 8 denoting the highest level of fastness. These fastness ratings are included in the summary charts at the ends of Chapters 5 and 7.

DEPTH OF SHADE

This is always measured as a percentage of weight of cloth, with the strongest shade usually around 8%. However, depending on the colour, type of dyestuff, and fabric, 3–6% strength will usually give a good, strong colour. 'Exhaust dyeing' is the term given to a dye-bath in which *all* the dye is absorbed by the cloth, leaving the remaining water clear, although this doesn't happen very often. However, use as small a percentage as possible to achieve the required colour, as excess dye will not be absorbed, take a long time to wash out and therefore be wasted. A very pale shade can be as low as 0.01% or even less (especially with reactive dyes).

Normally dyes are presumed to be at a standard strength of 100%. However, sometimes manufacturers make dyes up in a concentrated form, i.e. 125%, 150%, 200% or 300%, and this needs to be taken into account when calculating the amount of dyestuff needed. For example, if you use a 300% dye, it will be three times as strong as a standard strength dye, and you will only need a third as much to achieve the same shade.

ACID DYE-BATHS

Different acid dye-baths requires varying levels of acidity, and this is measured as a pH value and is given at the beginning of each recipe. To measure the pH accurately, you will need some pH testing paper, available from chemical and laboratory suppliers. The pH of the dye-bath should be tested when all of the assistants have been added, but without the dye liquor. An acid bath should always be neutralised before pouring down the drain.

WEIGHING SMALL QUANTITIES OF DYES, AUXILIAIRES AND CLOTH

This also applies to mixing up print pastes. If you do not have precision scales (i.e. without tens or hundredths of a gram calibrations), then those that measure in 1g increments may be sufficient for your needs. The drawback of scales that only weigh whole grammes, is that 100% accuracy will not be possible. For example, 1.4g of dye will show as 1g, or 10.8g cloth will show as 10g. Weighing in this way may well be adequate

Mary Ann Chatterton (UK)
Bolster and throw; reactive dyed and discharge printed antique French linen/ hemp with felt
Bolster: 91cm x 48cm; throw: 140cm x 205cm
Photo: Shannon Tofts

enough for most practitioners; for those who require exactitude then it really is worth investing in a set of precision scales.

NOTE:

- If the weight of your cloth *exceeds* the range on your scales, measure and cut a narrow strip (say 5cm) from selvedge to selvedge, weigh and then calculate the weight of the whole piece of cloth. If you do use this method, then keep a note of the weights of different cloths, and base all further dyeing on these amounts. Any weight of cloth inaccuracy will be especially noticeable on small samples dyed at anything less than full strength

The following describes a method of obtaining small quantities of dye as accurately as possible without using precision scales. You will need a plastic or Pyrex measuring cylinder, with 1ml graduations, and, if possible, a syringe graduated at 0.1ml.

The procedure is based upon making up a dye solution at a given strength. In the main, a 1% solution is the most convenient. This is made by dissolving 1g dye in 100ml water, or 2g dye in 200ml water and so on, always retaining the same ratio of dye to water. It is important to ensure that the amount of solution required is *feasible to measure accurately with the equipment available*. This may mean that a smaller quantity of dye needs to be dissolved in a greater quantity of water, resulting in a weaker solution of, say 0.1%. However, in some circumstances a very weak solution of 0.01% might be more appropriate. As a guide:

- for quantities of dye that are over say, 0.05g, a dye solution could be made at **1%** strength; this means that **1g dye is dissolved in 100ml water.** Note: for amounts of dye over 1g, it will be necessary to dissolve 2g in 200ml or 3g in 300ml etc. to create enough dye solution to measure from.
- for quantities of dye that are under say, 0.05g, a dye solution could be made at **0.1%** strength; this means that **1g dye is dissolved in 1000ml water.**
- for very pale colours on small or light pieces of fabric, it may be necessary to make a really weak solution of **0.01%, that is 1g dye dissolved in 10,000ml water** – see silk organza example below.

Having done this, the correct amount of solution can be calculated and measured in order to dye a small piece of cloth.

For example, to sample dye (cold water reactive) Red MX-8B at full strength (8%) on a piece of habotai silk that weighs 16g, the calculation would be as follows:

weight of cloth = 16g x 8% (8 ÷ 100) =
1.28g dyestuff;

So, having weighed 2g Red MX-8B and dissolved it in *200ml* water (1% solution), the correct quantity of solution can be calculated:

1.28g dye x 100ml water
= **128ml** dye solution.

To dye the same habotai silk Red MX-8B at 0.15%, the calculation would be:

weight of cloth = 16g x 0.15% (0.15 ÷ 100)
= 0.024g dyestuff.

So, having weighed 1g Red MX-8B and dissolved it in *1000ml* water (0.1% solution), the correct quantity of solution can be calculated:

0.024g dye x 1000ml water
= **24ml** dye solution.

A cloth like silk organza may only weigh a very small amount, and can be awkward if dyeing a pale shade; for example:

weight of cloth = 3g x 0.08% (0.08 ÷ 100)
= 0.0024g dyestuff, and
solution required = 0.0024g x 1000ml I
= **2.4ml**.

This quantity might still be too difficult to measure, especially if a graduated syringe is not available, so the dye solution *could* be made to a **0.01%** strength, so that 1g dye is dissolved in *10,000ml (10l)* water, resulting in the following:

0.0024g dye x 10,000ml
= **24ml** dye solution.

NOTE:
- It is very important to remember that the quantity of dye solution measured is *not in addition* to the total water quantity in the dyebath. Calculate and measure out the dye solution needed, deduct this from the total water

SUCCESSFUL DYEING

- Make sure that your cloth is in a prepared state (see Chapter 4)
- Always weigh cloth and weigh out dyes and other ingredients accurately
- Have adequate water to allow free movement of cloth, but not an excessive amount
- Follow temperature instructions for each recipe carefully, increasing temperatures *gradually* when required to do so
- Ensure that cloth is properly 'wetted-out' before dyeing commences. This is generally done by putting cloth into a prepared dye-bath *before* any other ingredients are added (there are some exceptions). Some fabrics may benefit from the addition of a 'wetting-out agent', eg. 'Matexil WA-KBN' to the dye-bath
- Assorted fabrics dyed in the same dye-bath may result in colours that differ from those achieved by dyeing cloth individually
- The dissolved dyestuff is referred to as 'dye liquor'. Check that dyestuff is properly dissolved, by pouring dye liquor back and forth between two stainless steel jugs. Remember that whatever the dye liquor quantity, it should be deducted from the overall water volume, so you are not adding extra water to the dye-bath
- Always *remove the cloth from the dye-bath before adding dye liquor* or each dye-bath assistant, taking care not to spill any liquid (except with vat dyes, where the cloth must remain below the surface). Always add acid to water and not the other way around, to avoid rising fumes
- Ensure that dye liquor and dye-bath assistants are properly dissolved and dispersed into the dye-bath before replacing cloth
- Keep the cloth moving throughout the dyeing process. If the dye-bath is not too hot, moving around with your hands (in gloves) is best. Otherwise, use a rod or stick, but make sure the end is rounded to prevent damage to fibres and that it can be cleaned easily; wood will stain and may affect the next dye-bath
- It is difficult to judge the colour of the cloth in the dye-bath as it will always appear darker; you will not know the *true* colour until the very end of the process once the cloth is washed and dried
- Be patient during washing out; ensure *all* excess dye is removed at the cold water stages
- For protein fibres dyed at high temperatures (i.e. wool and silk), it is important to *gradually* reduce the temperature of the dye-bath after dyeing and during washing out, so as not to 'shock' the fibres – wool may felt and silk lose its lustre
- After dyeing, always rinse cloth straight away. If dyed cloth is left soaking in cold (or hot) water for any length of time, streaking will occur, with colours separating where a colour mix was used. These marks can be difficult to remove, but washing at 60°C (140°F) with biological powder in an automatic machine may rectify the situation
- After the first cold rinse, it can be helpful to spin excess water out of the cloth to enable the hot wash to be as effective as possible, particularly with larger quantities of cloth
- After rinsing, ensure that cloth is well spun before hanging up (except wool or very delicate fabrics), as cloth that is too wet is also prone to streaking as it dries

quantity required, and measure the remainder of water into the dye-bath.

You may wish to keep dye solutions for future use; they should be stored in sealed containers and labelled clearly with the date and recipe, eg. 'direct Blue 2GD 1% solution'. The exception to this is with cold water reactive dyes, which once dissolved start to lose their strength and should be used immediately. A hot water reactive could be kept in solution for about three weeks before it started to lose strength, with other dye types in solution having a longer life-span. If in doubt, check with the manufacturer.

Some dyestuff solutions can be misleading, leaving you wondering whether you may have mis-weighed one of the ingredients. For example, in a green mix, one of the colours may appear more dominant. This may also be the case part of the way through the dyeing process, with the cloth initially taking up more yellow than blue. During washing out, it may be repeated, with a great deal of yellow running out first, then after the hot wash, the excess blue.

DYEING AT HIGH TEMPERATURES

As many dyes require to be heated during the dyeing process, it is important to maintain a satisfactory water volume. Depending on the temperature, dye liquor will evaporate and need to be 'topped up' to ensure there is adequate water covering the cloth – always add water of the same temperature to that in the dye-bath. Placing a lid over the dyeing vessel may help to minimise evaporation, but it makes agitation difficult. It is very important to ensure you have good ventilation when heating dye-baths at high temperatures; wear a fume mask if necessary.

USING A WINCH DYER

- It is helpful to know the maximum quantity of water the winch dyer will take; a small dyer like the one illustrated, takes a maximum of about 150 litres and dyes up to approximately 15m medium-weight linen. Covering the heating elements may take about 50 litres of water, and you will need much more than this to allow free movement of cloth above the protective plate. Exact desired quantity will, of course, depend on type of cloth.

▲ Winch dyer with 150 litre capacity
Joanna Kinnersly-Taylor (UK) ▶
Table linen, 2000
Screen-printed Irish linen

40

- Check water temperature is correct for your recipe. When dyeing with reactive cold water dyes, switch off the elements once the water has reached 30°C (86°F), to replicate sample dyeing conditions (except with turquoise).
- Some dyers are designed so that you can sew the cloth together *before* putting it in the machine, which makes life much easier. Others are completely enclosed and mean you have to join the cloth in situ. Take care when feeding cloth through to keep the ends dry to ease sewing. Ensure that there is no twist in the cloth.
- Sew the ends of your cloth together using double thickness thread to make large running stitches. Sew at least 4cm in from the ends.
- Run the cloth through the dyer for a few minutes to ensure it is thoroughly wetted-out and turning evenly.
- When adding dye liquor and subsequent dye-bath additives, you will need to temporarily switch off the winch. Get someone to hold back the bulk of the cloth so that you can add ingredients directly into the water without touching the exposed cloth. Even if the winch dyer *does* allow you to remove sewn cloth, it is not usually feasible to easily remove large quantities of cloth without spillage. Pour the dye liquor into the dye-bath carefully but quickly, swishing the jug around in the water to help disperse the dye. It is at this crucial point that any undissolved or lumpy dye will wreak havoc! Immediately switch the winch on again. Initially, the cloth will appear streaky, as some parts react more quickly than others, but after 5 or 10 minutes, the cloth will take on a more even tone.
- You will need to keep a watchful eye during the dyeing process, to make sure the cloth is being fed through properly and not gathering up

more on one side, or that it has caught somewhere and has stopped moving altogether.
- Tie long hair back and keep loose clothing and jewellery away from moving parts. *Always* switch off the elements at the end of the dyeing process and *before* emptying water.
- If you use a winch dyer with disperse, acid or reactive dyes (for wool), it may not be possible to bring the dye-bath to boiling point. This is because the action of the winch constantly introduces cold air into the dyer and the temperature will not normally rise above about 94°C (201°F), although this may vary depending on the type of machine.
- There may be some fabrics which are not possible to dye in a winch dyer, such as stiff linens and calicos. Although they may have been scoured and prepared in the normal way, they do not absorb enough water to allow themselves to be fed through the dye-bath, instead remaining static whilst the winch turns.
- The winch dyer is also a useful vessel for manual dyeing, (without utilising the winch), as it combines large water capacity with a means of heating.

RECIPES

The following dye recipes assume that you are starting with a prepared dye-bath with correct water quantity and at the right temperature, in which your cloth has already been wetted-out (except where stated otherwise). Read notes on 'Successful dyeing' before commencing.

Each recipe is preceded by a list of key information and includes washing-out instructions. There is also a summary of the dyeing recipes in chart form at the end of this chapter.

Dyeing with reactive cold water dyes

for cellulose fibres, silk, viscose rayon and nylon

LIQUOR RATIO: 20:1

TEMPERATURE: *start at:* 30°C (86°F)
(> 60°C (140°F) for turquoise).

ASSISTANTS: common salt (*or* Glauber's salt for turquoise), sodium carbonate.

DYEING TIME: 60 minutes (may be extended to 2 hours 20 minutes).

WASHING OUT: cold until clear / hot water (at least 85°C (185°F) for 2–3 minutes with 2ml Metapex 26 per litre water / cold until clear.

These dyes are highly reactive, taking their name from their ability to form a covalent bond with cellulose fibres resulting in excellent washing and lightfastness properties. Known as cold water dyes, the dye-bath is set at 30°C (86°F) (hand-hot) and does not therefore need to be heated through the dyeing period, making it very convenient in a studio situation. The exception to this is when using a turquoise, eg. Procion Turquoise MX-G, when the dye-bath must to be heated to 60°C (140°F) for the last 20 minutes of the dyeing process. It may also be preferable to substitute common salt with Glauber's salt when using turquoise or some other blues – check with the manufacturer's information.

I have successfully used the recipe that follows for dyeing silk, despite it being a protein fibre. As silk is very alkali-resistant (four times more than wool), using sodium carbonate as a fixative is acceptable. Colours may be more subdued on certain silks, and much paler on nylon compared with dyeing using acid dyes. There are recipe variations which use Glauber's salt instead of common salt, which can help slow the dyeing rate and

Mary Ann Chatterton (UK)
Stole; reactive dyed and discharge printed viscose fringe and antique French linen/hemp with felt
215cm x 80cm
Photo: Shannon Tofts

result in more even dyeing with certain colours on silk (check with manufacturer). Vinegar at the penultimate cold rinse helps neutralise any alkali remaining in the fibres and improves the handle of the silk, if it appears dull or hard.

NOTE:

* Do not use water above a temperature of 30°C (86°F) to assist in dissolving cold water reactive dyestuffs

METHOD:

1 Add the dye liquor to dye-bath, stirring thoroughly. Enter *wetted-out* cloth.

2 In the next 20 minutes, add salt in 3 equal portions, removing cloth each time. This is calculated as follows:

Depth of shade:

up to 0.5%= 30g salt per litre water

0.5 – 2%   = 40g salt per litre water

2 – 4%   = 50g salt per litre water

4 – 8%   = 60g salt per litre water

3 After this initial 20 minute period, remove cloth and add sodium carbonate in one portion, calculated as follows:

Depth of shade:

up to 0.5% = 3g sod. carb. per litre water

0.5 – 2%   = 4g sod. carb. per litre water

2 – 4%   = 7g sod. carb. per litre water

4 – 8%   = 10g sod. carb. per litre water

4 Re-enter cloth and continue dyeing for a further 40 minutes.

NOTES:

• On some fabrics, deep colours may be more difficult to obtain; if this is the case, the fixation period may be extended from 40 minutes for up to 2 hours – always do a test piece first

• If dyeing silk, you may wish to neutralise fibres to restore the lustre; add a tablespoon of vinegar to the penultimate cold rinse

Dyeing with reactive cold water dyes

or wool

LIQUOR RATIO: 20:1

TEMPERATURE: *start at:* 15°C (59°F) > 50°C (122°F) > 100°C (212°F).

ASSISTANTS: acetic acid, leveller (dye manufacturer's own or a pH neutral detergent).

pH value: 4.5–5

DYEING TIME: 65 minutes.

WASHING OUT: warm water until clear / warm water with 2ml Metapex 26 per litre water for 3 minutes / warm water.

Reactive dyes can also be used to dye wool, but have to be heated to a higher temperature. Because wool is a protein fibre and needs an acid dye-bath, salt and sodium carbonate are replaced with acetic acid. Colours are likely to be paler than those achieved by using acid dyes.

METHOD:

1 Add the following dye-bath assistants to the dye-bath:

acetic acid (20%) calculated as follows:

Depth of shade:

up to 0.5% = 3% acid on dry weight of cloth

0.5 – 2%   = 5% acid on dry weight of cloth

2 – 4%   = 7% acid on dry weight of cloth

4 – 8%   = 10% acid on dry weight of cloth

and a suitable leveller at 1% on dry weight of fabric.

2 Test the pH of the dye-bath and adjust accordingly.

3 Add the dye liquor to dye-bath, stirring thoroughly.

4 Enter *wetted-out* cloth to dye-bath and note the time dyeing started.

5 *Gradually* heat the bath so that it reaches 50°C (122°F) in 30 minutes. It is the steady, slow increase in heat that will result in more even dyeing and help prevent the wool from felting.

6 Continue dyeing at 50°C (122°F) for a further 30 minutes, then bring to the boil for 5 minutes to fix the dye.

7 Remove the dye-bath from heat and allow the cloth to cool down enough to handle.

Dyeing with reactive hot water dyes

for cellulose fibres, viscose rayon, silk and nylon

LIQUOR RATIO: 20:1

TEMPERATURE: *start at:* 40°C (104°F) > 80°C (176°F).

ASSISTANTS: common salt, sodium carbonate.

DYEING TIME: 75 minutes.

WASHING OUT: boil for 2 minutes (except silk, which should not be exposed to temperatures exceeding 85°C (183°F)) with 2ml Metapex 26 per litre water / cold water until clear.

Because these dyes are manufactured more particularly for *printing* and are less reactive in a dyeing

Dawn Dupree (UK)
'Grid', 2000
Dyed, screen-printed and painted with direct dyes on furnishing satin stretched on wooden frames –
30.5cm x 30.5cm each
Photo: FXP

situation, they must be dyed at higher temperatures and under more alkaline conditions. The increased alkaline environment may be damaging to some silks. Fastness properties of hot water dyes are similar to the cold water variety. The higher temperatures required for dyeing prohibit their use in the presence of wax resist techniques.

NOTE:

- Do not use water above a temperature of 70°C (158°F) to assist in dissolving hot water reactive dyestuffs

METHOD:

1 Calculate the amount of salt required as follows:

Depth of shade:

up to 0.5% = 40g salt per litre water
0.5 – 2% = 60g salt per litre water
2 – 4% = 80g salt per litre water
4 – 8% = 100g salt per litre water

Add **half** the salt to the dye-bath and immerse cloth, allowing it to become completely saturated with the salt solution.

2 Remove the cloth and add the dye liquor to dye-bath, stirring thoroughly.
3 Re-enter the wetted-out cloth to dye-bath and note the time dyeing started.
4 During the next 30 minutes, add the other half of the salt in 3 equal portions, removing the cloth each time.
5 Weigh out the sodium carbonate, calculated at 20g per litre of water, remove cloth and add to dye-bath.
6 Over the next 15 minutes, raise the dye-bath temperature to 80°C (176°F) and continue dyeing at this temperature for a further 30 minutes.

NOTES:

- This fixation period can be increased to achieve a deeper shade; always do a test sample first
- If dyeing silk, you may wish to neutralise fibres to restore the lustre; add a tablespoon of vinegar to the penultimate cold rinse

Dyeing with reactive hot water dyes

or wool

It is possible to dye wool using reactive hot water dyes, but much paler colours will be achieved, although duration of dyeing may be increased to increase depth of shade. A suitable levelling agent is required to promote even dyeing. Follow the recipe for cold water dyes for wool, with the exception of the dye-bath temperature, which, at step 5, should be gradually increased to reach 80°C (176°F) in 30 minutes. As with silk, remember to wash in gradually reducing water temperatures.

Dyeing with direct dyes

for cellulose, silk and viscose rayon

LIQUOR RATIO: 20:1

TEMPERATURE: *start at:* 40°C (104°F) > 90°C (194°F) (except silk 85°C (183°F)).

ASSISTANTS: common salt (or Glauber's salt for some colours).

DYEING TIME: 65 minutes +

WASHING OUT: cold until clear / hot (85°C (185°F) minimum) with 2ml Metapex 26 per litre water, for 5 minutes x 2 for deep colours / cold until clear.

The name for this group of dyes arose from the fact that the dyes possessed direct substantivity for cellulosic fibres, i.e. without the necessity for a pre-mordanting treatment. They are also suit-

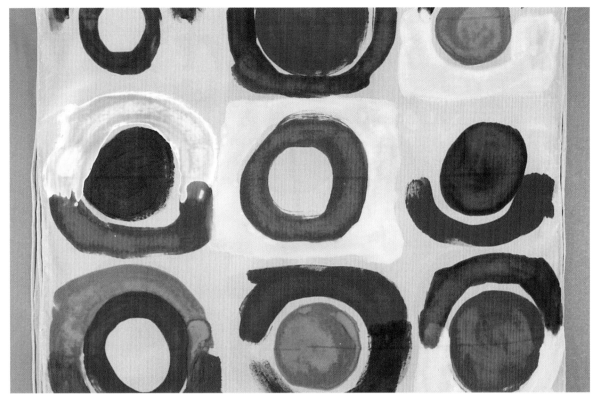

Frances Stevenson (UK)
Hand-painted with reactive dyes, reactive colour discharge and discharge on silk crêpe

using colours that fall into this category. Because direct dyes have to be used at high temperatures, they are unsuitable for wax resist processes.

able for silk. There is a good colour range available and they are often used to dye a dischargeable background colour; direct dyes are also cheaper than reactives. Although some colours show very good resistance to light, their washfastness is generally poor. This means that care needs to be taken at the washing out stage to ensure dye does not bleed and fix into unprinted areas. They should also not be used in a situation where frequent washing will take place. There are, however, certain fixatives available, which will slightly improve washfastness properties, and these are applied after the final rinse; consult dye manufacturer for advice. It is also important to be aware that many dyes in this group are known to be carcinogenic; if at all possible, avoid

METHOD:

1 Add the dye liquor to dye-bath, stirring thoroughly. (If you have difficulty in dissolving direct dyestuff, the dye liquor can be gently heated).

2 Work out the amount of salt required, calculated as follows:

Depth of shade:
up to 0.5% = 10% salt on dry weight of fabric
0.5 – 2%   = 20% salt on dry weight of fabric
2 – 4%   = 30% salt on dry weight of fabric
4 – 8%   = 40% salt on dry weight of fabric

and add the **first third** of salt to the dye-bath.

3 Enter the *wetted-out* cloth to the dye-bath and note the time dyeing started.

47

4 Dye for 5 minutes, remove the cloth and then add the **second third** of salt.

5 Continue dyeing, raising temperature *gradually* over the next 30 minutes to approximately 90°C (194°F) (except for silk, where the temperature should not exceed 85°C (183°F)).

6 Remove cloth once again, add the remaining salt, re-enter cloth and continue dyeing at this temperature for a further 30 minutes.

7 Remove dye-bath from heat, but continue agitating cloth until dye liquor cools enough to handle comfortably (between 30°–40°C (86°–104°F)).

NOTES:
- If dyeing silk, remember to gradually reduce water temperature at rinsing stages
- Also with silk, you may wish to neutralise fibres to restore the lustre; add a tablespoon of vinegar to the penultimate cold rinse

Dyeing with vat dyes

for cellulose fibres (except jute) and viscose rayon

LIQUOR RATIO: 30:1

TEMPERATURE: *start at:* 30°C (86°F) > 60°C (140°F).

ASSISTANTS: Metapex 26, methylated spirits or glycerine (for powders), sodium hydroxide solution 66° Tw (36°Bé) sodium hydrogen sulphite (hydrosulphite), Glauber's salt; for wet development: hydrogen peroxide, sodium bicarbonate.

DYEING TIME: 60 minutes.

OXIDISING: in air: up to 24 hours *or* in chemical bath (wet development): 15 minutes.

WASHING OUT: cold / hot (95°–100°C (203°–212°F)) with 2ml Metapex 26 per litre water for 5–20 minutes / cold until clear.

Vat dyes do not dissolve in water but release colour when oxygen is removed from the dye-bath, changing the chemical form. This process is called 'reduction', with the dye being transformed to its 'leuco' form (from the Greek leukos, meaning white). There are two groups of synthetic vat dyes – 'indigoid' (based on indigo) and 'anthraquinoid' (developed from anthracine, a coaltar product). Both are used in a neutral or alkaline dye-bath and have to be re-oxidised after dyeing to develop their full colour and to fix the dye. Indigoid vat dyes are more suitable on fibres that are alkali-sensitive; whereas the anthraquinoid dyes require a more alkaline dye-bath. This makes them particularly appropriate for cotton and linen, and as these fibres are often subjected to heavier laundering, the superior fastness properties of anthraquinoid dyes are also advantageous. Vat dyes come in powder, liquid or granular form, depending on the colour, although powders are less common nowadays. As a powder, the dye has to be pasted by sprinkling dye onto a small amount of methylated spirits or glycerine. The liquid may be a weaker preparation, typically 10–20% dyestuff in water with a small amount of dispersing agent; the grains also contain a little dispersing agent, together with a solid dilutant. There are various dyeing recipes for vat dyes and the exact procedure will depend on the manufacturer's recommendations. The recipe that follows is suitable for 'Duranthrene' (anthraquinoid) vat dyes.

NOTES:
- This recipe requires the sodium hydroxide solution to be at a specific gravity or viscosity

Amie Adelman (USA) ▶
'Controlling Hand' (detail), 1998
Vat dyed, screen-printed and painted discharge on canvas – 173cm x 235cm

and this is measured with a hydrometer using the Twaddell (°Tw) or Baumé (°Bé) scales

- Ensure this process is carried out in a well-ventilated area and wear suitable protective clothing
- If the cloth is bulky, adjust the water ratio slightly to allow the cloth to remain sub-merged at all times during the dyeing process; some small penny weights (available from haberdashers) stitched to the edges of the cloth will also help to achieve this

METHOD:

1 In a separate vessel, soak the cloth in warm water with a little Metapex 26 detergent. If you are dyeing a resist-printed cloth, it is best to leave it dry.

2 Weigh the dye, paste if necessary and gradually add a quantity of warm water that amounts to about 100 times that of the dye (e.g. 2g dye would require 200ml water) stirring well.

3 Measure out the following ingredients in the quantities required as shown, *carefully* adding one at a time to the dye-bath and stirring well to ensure thorough dissolution and even dispersal.

Depth of shade:
    0.1–1%   1–3%   3–5%   5–7%
Quantity per litre water:
sodium hydroxide solution:
    5–6ml   6–8ml   8–10ml   10–12ml
sodium hydrogen sulphite:
    1–1.5g   1.5–2g   2–2.5g   2.5–3.5g

NOTE:

- Sodium hydroxide (caustic soda) quantities, whilst relating to depth of shade, may also depend on the colour of dye. In the main, yel-lows, oranges and browns need more than blues, violets, greens and reds, but always check with manufacturer

Holly Reynolds (UK)
One-off square scarf
Printed, painted and stencilled chiffon satin silk with acid and vat dyes and discharge

4 Slowly add the dye solution to the dye-bath, stirring well.

5 Remove the cloth from its detergent bath and wring out by hand, or gently spin dry, before slowly lowering it into the prepared dye-bath, creating as few air bubbles as possible.

6 Over the next 30 minutes, gradually raise the temperature of the dye-bath to 60°C (140°F).

7 After this time, add *half* the Glauber's salt calculated as follows (do not remove the cloth):

Depth of shade:
0.1–1% 1–3% 3–5% 5–7%
Quantity per litre water:
Glauber's salt
8–10g 10–18g 18–26g 26–34g

and continue dyeing for a further 10 minutes, before adding the remaining half.

8 Retain the dye-bath at a temperature of 60°C (140°F) for the final 20 minutes.

9 After this period, remove the cloth from the dye-bath and oxidise in one of the following ways:

AIR: hang up immediately (over a bath or sink), with as few creases as possible and leave for several hours or overnight, for optimum results. The oxidisation will start to take effect as soon as the cloth comes into contact with the air.

or

CHEMICAL BATH: First rinse in water at 30° with a little sodium bicarbonate to help reduce the pH value then soak in a bath of water at 30°–60°C (86°–140°F) with 2–4ml hydrogen peroxide (6%) per litre water for 15 minutes.

Dyeing with basic dyes

Although basic dyes work on silk and wool in a similar way to acid dyes, their wash and lightfastness properties are very poor. However, for acrylic, they may be worth considering as this fibre can be difficult to dye; fastness properties are also improved with acrylic. These dyes are known to be carcinogenic. A dyeing recipe is not included in this book.

Dyeing with acid dyes

for wool, silk, jute, sisal and nylon

The dyes within this group have a natural affinity for protein fibres without the need for a mordant; they are also suitable for dyeing sisal and nylon. There are three main types of acid dyes; levelling, milling and metal-complex; a further sub-class is super-milling. Metal-complex are divided into two groups: 1:1 (1 metal atom to 1 dye molecule) and 1:2 (1 metal atom to 2 dye molecules). The recipe for 1:1 requires a very strong acid dye-bath, making it unsuitable in a studio situation and is therefore not included in this book.

Each group has good wash and lightfastness properties; see chart for fastness ratings. There are variations in colour ranges, and in the dye-bath assistants each dye type requires. For levelling agents, best results will be achieved by using the dye manufacturer's recommended product; however, a pH neutral detergent may be used instead. Remember with all these recipes to wash out wool and silk in gradually reducing temperatures of water.

Levelling (also known as fast dyes):

Strong, bright colours, which mix well together to give a wide colour range and produce very even dyeing. Levelling dyes have less affinity to protein fibres than the milling variety, and therefore need a more acidic dye-bath.

LIQUOR RATIO: 30:1

TEMPERATURE: *start at:* 50°C (122°F) > 100°C (212°F) (except silk 85°C (183°F)).

ASSISTANTS: Glauber's salt, acetic acid

pH value: 3–4

DYEING TIME: 60 minutes.

WASHING OUT: warm until clear / hot (85°C (185°F)) with 2ml Metapex 26 per litre water for 10 minutes / warm until clear. Dry away from direct heat or sunlight.

METHOD:

1 Add the following dye-bath assistants to the dye-bath:

Glauber's salt at 10% of weight of cloth and acetic acid (at 20% strength) as follows:

Depth of shade:
up to 0.5% = 4% acid on dry weight of fabric
0.5 – 2%   = 6% acid on dry weight of fabric
2 – 4%   = 8% acid on dry weight of fabric
4 – 8%   = 12% acid on dry weight of fabric

2 Test the pH of the dye-bath and adjust accordingly.

3 Add dye liquor to dye-bath, stirring thoroughly.

4 Enter the *wetted-out* cloth and *gradually* heat the dye-bath so that it reaches boiling point over a period of 30 minutes (except for silk, where temperature should not exceed 85°C (183°F)).

5 Continue simmering at the boil for a further 30 minutes.

6 Remove dye-bath from heat and allow to cool sufficiently so that cloth can be handled before washing out.

Milling:

Limited range of bright colours with a tendency to dye unevenly. Milling dyes have a high affinity for protein fibres and therefore do not require such an acidic dye-bath as the levelling type.

◀ Victoria Richards (UK)
Dressing gown; 1999; screen-printed with direct dyes and discharge on silk velvet
Photo: Andrea Heselton

LIQUOR RATIO: 30:1

TEMPERATURE: *start at:* 50°C (122°F) > 100°C (212°F) (except silk 85°C (183°F)) > 95°C (203°F).

ASSISTANTS: Glauber's salt, acetic acid, leveller (dye manufacturer's own or a pH neutral detergent), *or* ammonium sulphate, leveller (some dyes)
pH value: 5.2–6.2

DYEING TIME: 80 minutes.

WASHING OUT: warm until clear / hot (85°C (185°F)) with 2ml Metapex 26 per litre water for 10 minutes / warm until clear. Dry away from direct heat or sunlight.

NOTE:
• Some dyes in the 'milling' category require an alternative dye-bath assistant. At step 1, Glauber's salt and acetic acid would be replaced by ammonium sulphate, at 4% of weight of cloth. It is important to check with manufacturer's instructions

METHOD:

1 Add the following dye-bath assistants to the dye-bath, in this order:

Glauber's salt at 10% of weight of cloth and acetic acid (at 20% strength) as follows:

Depth of shade:
up to 0.5% = 2% acid on dry weight of fabric
0.5 – 2%   = 4% acid on dry weight of fabric
2 – 4%   = 6% acid on dry weight of fabric
4 – 8%   = 8% acid on dry weight of fabric

And a suitable leveller at 1% on dry weight of fabric.

2 Test the pH of the dye-bath and adjust accordingly.

3 Enter the *wetted-out* cloth and maintain the dye-bath temperature at 50°C (122°F) for the next 10 minutes.

4 Remove cloth and add dye liquor to dye-bath, stirring thoroughly.

5 Re-enter cloth and continue dyeing at 50°C (122°F) for a further 15 minutes.

6 Then *gradually* raise the temperature to reach boiling point in 40 minutes, (except for silk, where temperature should not exceed 85°C (183°F))

7 Reduce to simmer at 95°C (205°F) and continue for a further 15 minutes.

8 Remove dye-bath from heat and allow to cool sufficiently so that cloth can be handled.

Super-Milling:

Tendency to dye unevenly; small range of bright colours. These dyes require an even weaker acid than the milling variety, so acetic acid is replaced by ammonium sulphate.

LIQUOR RATIO: 30:1

TEMPERATURE: *start at:* 50°C (122°F) > 95°C (203°F) (except silk 85°C (183°F)).

ASSISTANTS: ammonium sulphate, leveller (dye manufacturer's own or a pH neutral detergent) *or* acetic acid, Glauber's salt, leveller (some dyes)

pH value: 5.5–7

DYEING TIME: 95 minutes (can be reduced to 65 minutes for pale shades if required).

WASHING OUT: warm until clear / hot (85°C (185°F)) with 2ml Metapex 26 per litre water for 10 minutes / warm until clear. Dry away from direct heat or sunlight.

NOTE:

- For some colours it may be preferable to substitute ammonium sulphate with acetic acid (20% strength) at up to 6% on dry weight of cloth, and Glauber's salt at 10% on dry weight of cloth.

METHOD:

1 Add the following dye-bath assistants to the dye-bath:

ammonium sulphate as follows:

Depth of shade:

up to 0.5%	= 2%	ammonium sulphate on dry weight of fabric
0.5 – 2%	= 2–3%	ammonium sulphate dry weight of fabric
2 – 4%	= 3–4%	ammonium sulphate on dry weight of fabric
4 – 8%	= 4%	ammonium sulphate on dry weight of fabric

and a suitable leveller at 1% on dry weight of fabric.

2 Test the pH of the dye-bath and adjust accordingly.

3 Enter the *wetted-out* cloth and allow to soak for 10 minutes.

4 Remove cloth and add dye liquor to dye-bath, stirring thoroughly.

5 Re-enter cloth and *gradually* heat the dye-bath so that it reaches 95°C (205°F) over a period of 45 minutes (except for silk, where temperature should not exceed 85°C (183°F)).

6 Continue dyeing at this temperature for a further 40 minutes, (or can be reduced to 15 minutes for pale shades if required).

7 Remove dye-bath from heat and allow to cool sufficiently so that cloth can be handled.

Metal-complex 1:2:

A muted and limited colour range (especially blues), but can be combined with compatible super-milling dyes to achieve a wider palette. One advantage of a metal-complex 1:2 dye–bath, is that wool and silk may be dyed together and the same colour will be achieved on both fibres; they also have excellent wash and lightfastness. It is also worth noting that a deep black is obtainable on silk, wool and nylon using metal-complex 1:2 dyes. The dyeing process for metal-complex 1:2 dyes is the same as that for super-milling, so readers should follow the previous recipe.

Dyeing with disperse dyes

for cellulose acetates and tri-acetates, nylon, polyester, acrylic and some plastics

LIQUOR RATIO: 50:1

TEMPERATURE: *start at:* 50°C (122°F) > 100°C (212°F) > 90°–95°C (194°–203°F) (*or* for acrylic do not exceed 85°C (185°F)).

ASSISTANTS: pH neutral detergent, carrier (for polyester), acetic acid (optional).

DYEING TIME: 80 minutes.

WASHING OUT: warm (50°C (122°F)) with 2ml Metapex 26 per litre water for 5 minutes / cold until clear.

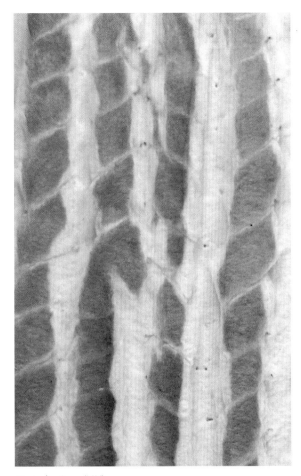

Natasha Lee (UK)
Stitch resist and heat transfer print with disperse dyes on fleece

Unlike other dyes, disperse dyes do not dissolve in water to form a solution. Instead the particles disperse in the water, penetrating the fibre when heated. A 'dispersing agent' is required to help even distribution of the dye, preventing it from sinking to the bottom of the dye-bath during the dyeing process. Whilst a pH neutral detergent or soap flakes as a dispersing agent works adequately, you may wish to use a proprietary compound recommended by the specific dye manufacturer.

Different fibre blends take up colour depending on their main constituent. For example, a nylon/acrylic mix accepts colour more readily than a wool/acrylic mix. Disperse dyes are useful for dyeing plastic items such as buttons and buckles. They have a moderate fastness to washing, dry-cleaning and light. Because synthetic fibres have a more open texture, a larger water ratio of 50:1 is required to allow for satisfactory immersion in the dye-bath.

Do not use dyeing vessels made from tin or aluminium for dyeing with disperse dyes. Disperse dyes-baths utilising a carrier (for polyester) give off very strong fumes; ensure there is adequate ventilation and wear a mask if necessary.

NOTES:

- If dyeing polyester, a carrier will be required to allow dye to penetrate its tight molecular structure. See Step 1 below.
- If washing acrylic, avoid excessive handling.
- Although I have used the following recipe successfully, other methods incorporate the use of acetic acid, and you may wish to experiment with this addition to see if it is preferable with certain fibre blends. The acid would be added to the dye-bath at Step 1 below.

METHOD:

1 Measure out the pH neutral detergent or soap flakes as dispersing agent at 1g per litre water and add to dye-bath. If dyeing polyester, also add appropriate carrier at this stage, calculated as follows:

Depth of shade:

up to 0.5%	= 6% carrier on weight of cloth
0.5 – 2%	= 8% carrier on weight of cloth
2 – 4%	= 10% carrier on weight of cloth
4 – 8%	= 12% carrier on weight of cloth

If incorporating acetic acid, this would also go into the dye-bath at this stage. The quantity would be 6% (at 20% strength) on weight of cloth.

2 Immerse cloth in the dye-bath and soak in dispersing agent solution for 10 minutes.

3 After weighing out dye, use a measuring jug and take out water from the dye-bath amounting to 8–10 times the weight of the dye, eg. if you have 10g of dye, you would need about 80–100ml water.

4 Gradually sprinkle the dye onto the surface of the water in the jug (do not add water to dye), allowing a few minutes for it to become completely dispersed. Stir thoroughly.

5 Remove cloth and add dye liquor to bath, stirring thoroughly. Re-enter the cloth and note the time dyeing started. Move the cloth gently to encourage even exposure to the dye.

6 Heat the dye-bath *gradually* so that it reaches boiling point in 30 minutes, then reduce the temperature to between 90°–95°C (194°–203°F) to avoid damaging the fibres. If dyeing more vulnerable acrylic fibres, reduce the temperature to 85°C (185°F) or less, to avoid damage and distortion.

7 Continue dyeing at this temperature for a further 40 minutes, moving the cloth very gently from time to time.

8 Remove the dye-bath from heat and allow fibres to cool down sufficiently to be handled.

NOTE:

- Disperse dyes leave a very stubborn residue in the dye-bath and it is important to thoroughly clean the dyeing vessel after use

Stripping dyed cloth

This is an unpleasant procedure and one that I would not particularly recommend. However, there may be an occasion when it is absolutely necessary to salvage an incorrectly dyed piece of cloth. Before starting, check that the dye to be stripped is removable. Because stripping is a severe process and the quality of the cloth may be impaired, stop when no further progress is apparent. It is important to undertake the stripping process in well-ventilated conditions and to wear a fume mask.

Cotton and linen

LIQUOR RATIO: 30:1

TEMPERATURE: *start at:* 50°C (122°F) > 70°C (158°F)

ASSISTANTS: ammonia, sodium hydrogen sulphite, sodium hypochlorite.

STRIPPING TIME: 10 minutes minimum, with additional time if progress made.

WASHING OUT: warm then cold water.

METHOD:

1 Make up a bath at 50°C (122°F) and carefully stir in 2ml ammonia (strength: 1 part ammonia to 1 part water) per litre water and 3g sodium hydrogen sulphite per litre water.

2 Immerse fabric into bath for a few minutes, then slowly raise the temperature to 70°C (158°F) to encourage stripping, but do not exceed this temperature.

3 If, after about 10 minutes, some of the colour has been removed but there appears to be no further progress, a further 3g of sodium hydrogen sulphite per litre water may be added. Agitate gently for another 15 minutes.

4 If sufficient colour is removed, take out cloth and rinse well in warm then cold water, neutralising if necessary, spin and dry.

5 However, if adequate colour has still not been removed, make up a further bath of cold water containing 20ml sodium hypochlorite at 4% strength (ordinary household bleach) per litre and immerse cloth for a few minutes.

6 Finally, rinse in a warm bath with a weak solution of ammonia and sodium hydrogen sulphite, rinse well in cold water, spin and dry.

Wool and silk

First of all, try the first half of the above method for cotton and linen. If this is unsuccessful, use the following method:

LIQUOR RATIO: 30:1

TEMPERATURE: *start at:* 50°C (122°F) > 85–100°C (185–212°F).

ASSISTANTS: Formosul, acetic acid.

STRIPPING TIME: time taken to reach required temperature, with additional time at the boil if progress made.

WASHING OUT: warm then cold water.

METHOD:

1 Make up a bath at 50°C (122°F) and carefully stir in 3.5g Formosul per litre water and 2ml acetic acid (at 33% strength) per litre water.

2 Immerse the fabric into bath, then slowly raise the temperature to 85–100°C (185–212°F). Continue at the boil until colour removal is complete or halts.

3 Rinse well in warm then cold water, neutralising if necessary, spin and dry.

NOTE:

• Whilst silk should not normally be exposed to temperatures exceeding 85°C (185°F), it may be necessary to bring the stripping bath to the boil to achieve colour removal. As the chemicals used in the stripping process can be detrimental to fibres, boiling silk may not cause any further damage than has already occurred

SUMMARY OF DYEING RECIPES

pH value	Fabric	Liquor ratio	Temperature range	Dye-bath assistants	Dyeing time	Washing out
Reactive: cold water	(washfastness: 5 out of 5			lightfastness: 5–6 out of 8)		
	cellulose fibres, silk, viscose rayon and nylon	20:1	start at: 30°C (86°F) (except turquoise: 60°C (140°)) these temperatures should not be exceeded	common salt (or Glauber's salt for turquoise), sodium carbonate	60 mins.; can extend to 140 mins. for certain shades if required	cold until clear / hot (85°C (185°F) + 2ml Metapex 26 per litre water 2–3 mins. / cold until clear
4.5–5	wool	20:1	15°C (59°F) > 50°C (122°F) > 100°C (212°F)	acetic acid, leveller	65 minutes	warm until clear / warm + 2ml Metapex 26 per litre 3 mins. / warm
Reactive: hot water	(washfastness: 5 out of 5			lightfastness: 5–6 out of 8)		
	cellulose fibres, silk, viscose rayon and nylon	20:1	40°C (104°F) > 80°C (176°F)	common salt sodium carbonate	75 minutes	boil 2 mins. (except silk: not above 85°C (183°F)) + 2ml Metapex 26 per litre water / cold until clear
4.5–5	wool	20:1	15°C (59°F) > 80°C (176°F) > 100°C (212°F)	acetic acid, leveller	65 minutes; can be extended for darker shades if necessary	warm until clear / warm + 2ml Metapex 26 per litre water 3 mins / warm
Direct:	(washfastness: 3–4 out of 5			lightfastness: 6 out of 8)		
	cellulose fibres, silk and viscose rayon	20:1	40°C (104°F) > 90°C (185°F) (except silk: 85°C (183°F))	common salt or Glauber's salt (some colours)	65 minutes +	cold until clear / hot (85°C (185°F) minimum) + 2ml Metapex 26 per litre water 5 mins. x 2 / cold until clear
Vat:	(washfastness: 4–5 out of 5			lightfastness: 6–7 out of 8)		
	cellulose fibres (except jute), and viscose rayon	30:1	30°C (86°F) > 60°C (140°F)	Metapex 26, methylated spirits, sodium hydroxide, sodium hydrogen sulphite, Glauber's salt, (+ hydrogen peroxide + sodium bicarbonate if oxidising in chemical bath)	60 minutes	cold / hot (95°–100°C (203°–212°F)) + 2ml Metapex 26 per litre water 5–20 mins. / cold until clear

pH value	Fabric	Liquor ratio	Temperature range	Dye-bath assistants	Dyeing time	Washing out
Acid: levelling			(washfastness: 4 out of 5		lightfastness: 4–5 out of 8)	
3–4	wool, silk, jute, sisal and nylon	30:1	50°C (122°F) > 100°C (212°F) (except silk: 85°C (183°F))	Glauber's salt, acetic acid	60 minutes	warm until clear / hot (85°C (185°F)) + 2ml Metapex 26 per litre water 10 mins. / warm until clear /
Acid: milling			(washfastness: 4 out of 5		lightfastness: 4–5 out of 8)	
5.2–6.2	wool, silk, jute, sisal and nylon	30:1	50°C (122°F) > 100°C (212°F) (except silk: 85°C (183°F)) > 95°C (203°F) (for silk, retain at 85°C (183°F))	Glauber's salt, acetic acid, leveller, or ammonium sulphate, leveller (check with manufacturer)	80 minutes	warm until clear / hot (85°C (185°F)) + 2ml Metapex 26 per litre water 10 mins. / warm until clear
Acid: super-milling			(washfastness: 4 out of 5		lightfastness: 4–5 out of 8)	
5.5–7	wool, silk, jute, sisal and nylon	30:1	50°C (122°F) > 95°C (203°F) (except silk: 85°C (183°F))	ammonium sulphate, leveller or Glauber's salt, acetic acid (for some dyes), leveller	95 minutes; (can be reduced to 65 minutes for pale shades)	warm until clear / hot (85°C (185°F)) + 2ml Metapex 26 per litre water 10 mins. / warm until clear
Metal-complex 1:2			(washfastness: 4–5 out of 5		lightfastness: 6–7 out of 8)	
5.5–7	wool, silk, jute, sisal and nylon	30:1	50°C (122°F) > 95°C (203°F) (except silk: 85°C (183°F))	ammonium sulphate, leveller or Glauber's salt, acetic acid (for some dyes), leveller	95 minutes; (can be reduced to 65 minutes for pale shades)	warm until clear / hot (85°C (185°F)) + 2ml Metapex 26 per litre water 10 mins. / warm until clear /
Disperse			(washfastness 5 out of 5		lightfastness: 6 out of 8)	
	cellulose acetates and tri-acetates, nylon, polyester, acrylic and some plastics	50:1	50°C (122°F) > 100°C (212°F) > 90°–95°C (194°–203°F) or for acrylic, do not exceed 85°C (185°F)	pH neutral detergent, carrier (for polyester), acetic acid (optional)	80 minutes	warm (50°C (122°F)) + 2ml Metapex 26 per litre water 5 mins. / cold until clear

CHAPTER SIX

THICKENERS

A THICKENER FORMS THE BASIS of all print pastes and is the vehicle to which all the other printing auxiliaries and dyestuffs are added. The choice of thickener depends upon type of dyestuff and cloth used, ability to withstand fixation without breaking down, and to wash out easily from the finished print, leaving no residue. As with dyeing, remember to use soft water in all recipes for thickeners and print pastes.

MIXING

Many thickeners need to be left to stand for a few hours or sometimes overnight before use, so it is best to mix enough for all the pots of print paste you will need in one session. Because it is important that the thickener has a smooth consistency, an electric hand whisk is extremely useful. For ease, 2–2.5 litres of thickener can be mixed at one time, unless you have an industrial or catering mixer that can cope with greater amounts. A 2.5 litre plastic tub with a lid is ideal for mixing and storing thickeners; alternatively for smaller amounts use a 1 litre plastic beaker.

LIFESPAN

Once mixed, thickeners should be kept in an airtight container and stored in a cool place, and as a general rule, used within about 4 weeks, as the consistency can deteriorate and mould can form. It is generally best to mix small quantities of

Jasia Szerszynska (UK)
Urban Landscape: Day
Screen-printed cotton and linen with pigment dyes
115cm x 300cm

thickeners and print pastes so that they are as fresh as possible and to minimise waste.

Ready-mixed emulsion thickeners have a much longer shelf life, but may need to be stirred thoroughly before use to re-blend any separated ingredients.

Rachael Howard (UK)
'Waters Edge' – from 'Sunbathers' series, 1999
Screen-printed cambric cotton, with machine embroidery and appliquéd silk and cotton – 46cm x 62cm
Photo: Small Works Photography

All the following recipes are based on mixing a quantity of thickener using 1 litre soft water; if living in a hard water area, a softener such as 'Calgon' should be added.

NATURAL GUMS

ALGINATES

Sodium alginate is found in most brown seaweeds and is used as a thickener for printing, as well as being widely used in the food industry. After the Second World War, alginate thickeners came to be utilised more fully, increasing in popularity in the late 1950s when reactive dyes were developed. This group of thickeners are particularly versatile and can be used with reactive, direct, and disperse dyes (Manutex F only). Print pastes made with an alginate thickener give smooth, level shades over large areas and allow the dye to penetrate deep into the fibres. After printing, the dried paste remains relatively supple so avoiding cracking prior to fixation. This thickener also washes out easily, returning the cloth to its original state.

Two of the most widely used alginates are marketed under the trade name 'Manutex' and different suppliers may suffix the name with a number or code. As with all recipes, there is variation in exact quantites of Manutex per litre water, and this can be adapted if necessary to suit personal preference depending on the end use.

MANUTEX F: has a high solid content and low viscosity, and makes it particularly suitable for printing on fine fabrics and chlorinated wool and where there is overprinting; it also gives very level prints. It is used with gum arabic to make table gum and is more expensive than Manutex RS.

MANUTEX RS: has a lower solid content and high viscosity and forms a flexible film after printing. It can be more suitable for hand-painting, thicker fabrics and where there is no overprinting.

Manutex F or Manutex RS thickener:

1 Measure 1 litre of cold water and add 2g of Milton (or other sterilising fluid).
2 Weigh out 143g Manutex F *or* 50g Manutex RS powder and create a 'vortex' in the water

using an electric whisk. Pour the powder quite fast into the vortex, and continue whisking for several minutes until the gum thickens. Leave to stand for 1½–2 hours to disperse any remaining lumps.

NOTE:

• The addition of a sterilising fluid, such as 'Milton', can help deter mould in Manutex thickeners

LOCUST BEAN GUMS

Also known as Gums Gatto or Carob Gum. Locust bean gums come from the long sweet pod (locust bean) produced by the carob tree and came into wide use in the 1970s. Gum is extracted from the seeds and treated to make it easily soluble in water. Because it is very stable in either alkaline or acidic conditions, it is a versatile gum and can be used with direct, acid and disperse dyes and is especially suitable for use on wool and silk. This gum is also used as a thickener in devoré paste for printing on cellulose fibres. There are various makes and grades of gum available, all of which vary in proportions of gum required. Indalca PA/3-R is the locust bean gum recommended for recipes in this book; it is also a very economical gum.

Indalca PA/3-R gum:

1 Measure 1 litre cold water and, stirring constantly, slowly sprinkle 100g Indalca PA/3-R powder onto the surface of the water. Leave to stand for 1–2 hours before use.

GUAR GUM

This is extracted from the guar plant and is very similar to locust bean gum; 'Lameprint A–14 Super' is one brand referred to in this book and now replaces 'Gum 301 Extra'. It can be used in acid and disperse pastes, discharge printing, some resist techniques and devoré printing onto cellulose fibres.

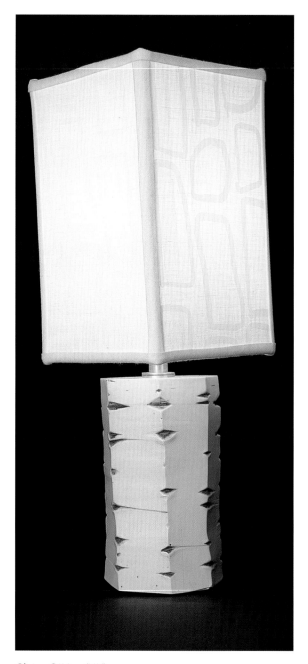

Claire O'Hea (UK)
'haiku' soft shade
Screen-printed pigment dye onto linen
Photo: Arturo Vilar

Lameprint A–14 Super:

1 Measure 1 litre cold water and, stirring constantly, slowly sprinkle 120g Lameprint A–14 Super onto the surface of the water. Leave to stand for 1–2 hours before use.

GUM TRAGACANTH

This gum, in its original form, was also known as 'Gum Dragon' or 'Devil's Toenails', due to its white to yellow scaly appearance and comes from the slits in the bark of the plant *Astragalus gummifer*. Available in powdered form, it can be used in direct and vat dye pastes.

1 Measure 1 litre warm water, and slowly sprinkle 75g Gum Tragacanth onto the surface, mixing thoroughly with an electric whisk. Leave to stand for 24 hours, stirring occasionally.

GUM ARABIC

This is one of the purer gums obtained from wounds in the bark of acacia trees and is also known as Gum Senegal. Traditionally, it was particularly effective for printing on silk, as it has a high solids content and achieves a sharp print and even colour, although not as deep in shade as pastes made with Gum Tragacanth or starch thickeners. However, the gum can be brittle when dry which can damage fragile cloth prior to fixation; British Gum is better in this respect. Making up gum arabic is a very time-consuming procedure and if preferred, it may be bought as a ready-mixed solution, its purity in this form helps to prevent it going off. Gum Arabic can be used with direct and acid dyestuffs.

1 In a heat-proof container, measure out 1 litre cold water and stir in 450g Gum Arabic crystals.

2 Bring to the boil and maintain at this temperature, stirring constantly, for 3 hours. Allow to cool, and then gradually add enough cold water to bring the volume to 1 litre, stirring all the time. Strain if necessary.

Table gum:

Gum arabic may also be combined with Manutex 'F' gum to make a table gum.

1 Weigh 100g pre-made Manutex 'F' gum into a 2 litre container and gradually whisk in the gum arabic solution made as above.

2 Allow to cool and stir in ½ teaspoon glycerine to prevent a crust forming.

CRYSTAL GUM

This gum is often known under its trade name of Nafka gum and is a very good substitute for gum arabic. It has a high solids content, contains no impurities and makes a very smooth even thickener especially suitable for acid print pastes, as well as in some direct and disperse pastes, although with the latter, problems may be experienced with washing out on some synthetics. Because of its high solubility, it gives good printing definition and is especially suitable for fine silks and delicate fabrics, where washing out is straightforward.

Crystal or 'Nafka' gum:

1 Measure 1 litre cold water and create a 'vortex' in the water using a whisk. Pour 200g Crystal gum powder quite fast into the vortex, and continue whisking for a minute or two.

2 Leave to stand overnight and then strain through a sieve to remove any remaining

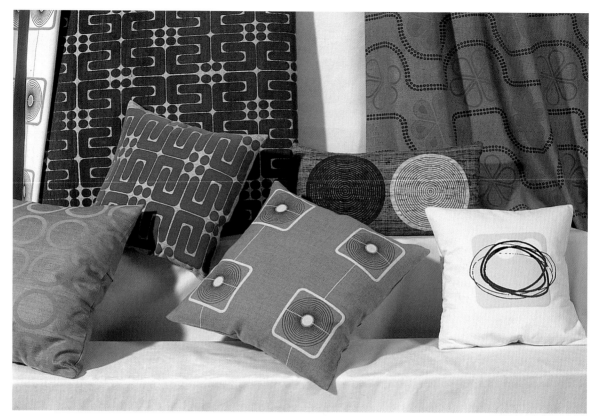

Double Helix (UK)
Cushions and fabric by the metre – flock and pigment printed silk, linen and velvet
Photo: Ruth Clark

lumps. If required for immediate use, it is possible to heat the solution to the boil for five minutes; and allow to cool before straining.

BRITISH GUM (DEXTRIN)

This starch is also known as dextrin and was developed about 150 years ago. The wheat or maize starch was pre-treated with acid, and then roasted at varying temperatures. As a result, several different qualities were obtained, which were suitable for various uses. British Gum can be used with vat and disperse dyestuffs and also as a resist paste, where it can produce a 'cracked' effect.

British Gum or dextrin

1 Weigh 1000g dextrin powder into a heat-proof container.
2 Slowly add 1 litre boiling water, stirring constantly to prevent lumps from forming.
3 Place the container with the mixed gum into a larger heat-proof vessel containing water (a *bain marie* or double boiler). Bring to the boil and simmer gently for 20 minutes, stirring constantly.
4 Allow to cool and strain the gum if necessary before use.

STARCH ETHERS

Solvitose C5 is a widely used modified starch, whereby the chemical properties have been altered to allow it to dissolve in water. As a starch ether, it can withstand strong alkaline conditions

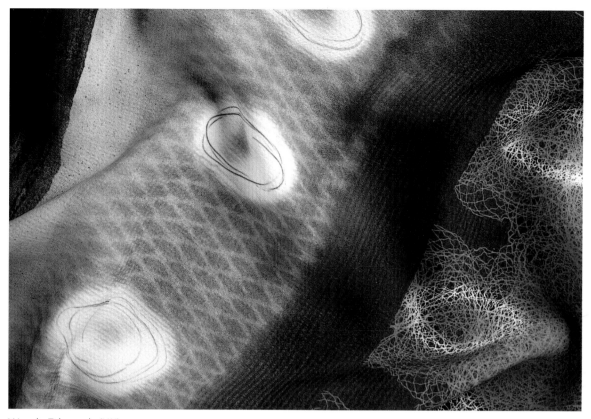

Wendy Edmonds (UK)
Scarf – filigree (detail) – Heat transfer print with
disperse dye on microfibre
Photo: Nick Turner

without breaking down. It is used for white discharge printing on reactive and direct grounds, colour discharge printing with basic dyes and colour discharge printing with pigments. It is also the thickener used for devoré printing onto protein fibres and in crimping paste. Solvitose C5 is the recommended starch ether thickener for recipes in this book.

Solvitose C5

1 Measure 1 litre cold water, and sprinkle 120g Solvitose C5 flakes onto the surface, mixing thoroughly with an electric whisk. Leave to stand for a few hours or, if possible, overnight.

CELLULOSE ETHERS

Cellulose ethers are made from purified cellulose of cotton or wood origin and may be used as thickeners which are capable of withstanding acidic conditions, for example, in acid and pigment resist pastes.

SYNTHETICS

EMULSION THICKENERS

These are now mostly used with pigment print pastes, where white spirit has mainly been replaced by solvent-free ingredients. In the past, white spirit emulsion was combined with an alginate thickener such as Manutex to make a thickener for use with reactive and disperse dyes. In industry their use has declined, due to environmental concern and the development of synthetic alternatives. Thickeners or binders for pigment pastes can be bought ready-mixed.

Joanna Kinnersly-Taylor (UK)
Wall-hangings sited at the 'Innovation Centre', Westlakes Science & Technology Park, Cumbria, 1998;
Eric Parry Architects; commissioned by Westlakes Properties Ltd and English Partnerships. Dyed, screen-printed, hand-painted and devoré, with reactive dyes and discharge on silk velvet – 400cm x 80cm each
Photo: Paul McMullin

CHAPTER SEVEN

PRINT PASTES – DIRECT STYLE

DIRECT STYLE IS often used to describe the printing of positive images with one or more coloured print pastes.

DEPTH OF SHADE

(see also 'The Colour Index' in Chapter 5.)

In mixing colours, the maximum amount of dyestuff required per 1000g of paste to achieve a full-strength shade varies from one dye group to another and this is given with each recipe. You may not need to mix a full strength shade very often, as a quarter-strength will usually still give a strong colour. If maximum strengths are exceeded, the cloth will be time-consuming to wash-out with dye being wasted.

Calculating the amount of dyestuff required is very simple. For example, to print a reactive navy blue at quarter-strength, (a full-strength reactive being 50g/1000g print paste):

50g Navy P-2R ÷ 4 = 12.5g dyestuff per 1000g print paste

and if you are only making 250g print paste: (i.e. a quarter of the above)

12.5g dyestuff ÷ 4 = 3.125g Navy P-2R.

If you are making a colour made up from three

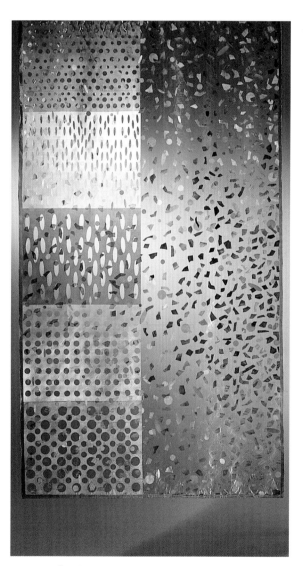

Jason Pollen (USA)
'One Windy Wednesday', 2000
Fused silk, metallic organza, reactive dye, pigment, printed and painted – 197.5cm x 112cm
Photo: Matthew McFarland, Kansas City

different dyes, the total amount of dye would still be 50g for a full-strength shade. For example a dark, pinky-red may be made up as follows:

		at quarter-strength:	
Violet P-3R	17g	4.25g	
Scarlet P-2R	31g total 50g	7.75g total 12.5g	
Blue SP-3R	2g	0.5g	

A very pale colour made with reactive dye, for example, may only need to be a hundredth of full strength, i.e. 0.5g dye per litre print paste. See Chapter 5 for advice on weighing small quantities of dye without precision scales.

MIXING AND CONSISTENCY

The thickness or viscosity of the print paste is one of the factors that can affect the quality of a screen print. Too runny a paste on a fine cloth, especially if the design is detailed, will lead to bleeding, whereas a very thick paste printed onto a heavyweight fabric may not penetrate the fibres properly. The type of squeegee, size of screen mesh, and number of pulls and pressure applied when printing are also important aspects of a successful print. All these things should be taken into consideration when mixing up the print paste.

Use as *little water as possible* to achieve proper dissolution of each ingredient. Use stainless steel containers, because the vessel can be heated directly (or stood in another container of boiling water) and ingredients come away easily from the surface. Some dyestuffs are easier to dissolve than others; sticky lumps may form, or undissolved residue may be left at the bottom of the jug. Pouring dye solution from one jug to an-

other is a good way of checking it has dissolved properly. Urea can also be difficult to dissolve; you will need to crush the granules against the side of the jug, or, if preferred, the solution may be heated gently to aid dissolution. Note that the urea solution quickly solidifies as it cools. Some printers prefer to mix the dry dyestuff and urea together first, before dissolving, and this can be helpful with certain colours. However, remember that some dyes should not be heated above a certain temperature.

It is important to add all dissolved auxiliaries and dyestuffs to the thickener *gradually*, mixing well between each addition, to ensure that the paste does not become too runny and each ingredient is properly dispersed. Do not worry if the paste is too thick for the required use once all the ingredients are mixed in, *water can gradually be added at the end until the desired consistency is achieved*. The recipes that follow are all based on this method, where the *exact* water quantity is left open. This is because there are several factors that will determine the amount of water needed: quantities of dry ingredients that are dissolved in appropriate amounts of water; ambient temperature; specific consistency depending on use etc. It is better to have a thicker paste that can be watered down than a paste that is too runny. Paste can also thicken if left for a period of time, particularly in extremes of temperature, and, again, water may be added to return paste to original viscosity. All types of print paste can be watered down to the required consistency for hand-painting onto cloth. A variety of implements can be used to apply the paste from brushes and rollers to sponges, pads and spray guns.

Once final print paste is mixed, it should be covered with cling film, or sealed in an airtight container, and labelled with the colour (cross-referenced in your dye notebook) and date.

RECIPES

At the beginning of each recipe, key information is given about print pastes made with dyes from that particular group, so that a summary of the whole process can be seen at a glance. Where a choice is given for thickeners, refer to Chapter 6 for the most suitable. Step by step instructions for mixing each type of paste are given, with extra notes and information for variations. Each recipe is based on starting with a given amount of thickener, usually 500–600g, which, once all the other ingredients are added, will make *up to* 1000g print paste depending on all the factors mentioned previously. Although this final quantity may not be as much as 1000g, the maximum strengths indicated are described, for example, as 50g dyestuff per 1000g paste, and do relate to a paste mixed in this way, with these amounts of thickener. However, if you are mixing sample colours, it is best to make a smaller quantity to start with, using 250g thickener, (a lesser amount than this makes the auxiliaries awkward to measure), to avoid waste.

COVERAGE

As a general guide, 500–750ml print paste, will print about 1m x 1.22m of medium-weight cloth with a half-tone design of about 65% coverage.

FIXING

Readers are reminded that all fixing method information given is only a guide, as variations will occur depending on the type of steaming or baking equipment used. Sampling and testing is paramount to achieve the best results.

Printing with reactive dyes (hot and cold water)

for cellulose, silk, wool (chlorinated is best) and viscose-rayon

THICKENER: alginates (Manutex F *or* Manutex RS)

AUXILIARIES: urea, oxidising agent (Matexil P-AL), sodium bicarbonate *or* sodium carbonate (variation when baking)

STRENGTHS: 0.5g–50g dye per 1000g paste

FIXING METHODS: saturated steaming at atmospheric pressure: 10–30 minutes (cold water types require less steaming) *or* baking: 150°C (302°F): 5–10 minutes (best results on mercerised cotton) *or* air fixing: cold water types only (see below).

WASHING OUT: cold water until clear 85°–100°C (185°–212°F) with 2ml Metapex 26 per litre for 5 minutes (x 2 for very deep colours) / cold until clear.

When used for printing onto cloth, reactive dyes form a covalent bond between dye and fibre, giving excellent washing and lightfastness properties. Cloth also retains its original texture, with a superior handle to pigment-printed fabrics, for example. Hot water dyes (such as Procion 'H' or 'P' types) are manufactured particularly for printing, producing excellent results with good fastness properties, and being less reactive than the cold water variety, are *best* fixed by steaming. It is possible to use *cold water* dyes for printing, but paste must be mixed and used on the same day; again steaming may be used as the fixation method here. Both types may also be fixed by baking, with slight alterations to the paste mix as follows:

- increase the urea content from 50g up to 200g per 1000g paste (test first)
- for the hot water dyes, substitute the sodium bicarbonate with 18g sodium *carbonate* per 1000g paste
- for the cold water type, reduce the quantity of sodium bicarbonate from 30g to 18g per 1000g paste

NOTES:
- When dissolving dyes, do not use water exceeding 70°C (158°F) (or 30°C (56°F) for cold water dyes)
- With both dye types, if fixing by baking, best results are achieved on mercerised cotton
- Do not mix hot and cold water dyes in the same recipe

The cold water variety may also be fixed by 'air fixing', although results will not be as good as cloth that is fixed by steaming. If this method is chosen, the following should be taken into account:

- substitute the 30g sodium bicarbonate per 1000g paste with 20g sodium bicarbonate *and* 10g sodium carbonate per 1000g paste

    alternatively

soak the (scoured) fabric in a bath of cold water containing 20g sodium carbonate per litre for 30 seconds. Squeeze the fabric, allow to dry and then iron.

Print using paste made with cold water dyes and dry by hanging in a warm, humid atmosphere for 24–48 hours. The washing out method is the same for steamed and baked fabrics.

OTHER VARIATIONS:

Printing on wool

As a rule, sodium bicarbonate is *not* required if printing on wool; in some cases it can result in lower colour yield by 10–15%, although in others, its addition, at 5–10g per 1000g paste, does improve results. Test first if unsure. Improvement in print quality may also be achieved by the addition of 50g glycerine per 1000g paste.

Printing on silk

On some fine silks like habotai, slight bleeding may occur; this can be alleviated by reducing the urea content substantially and also adding less water.

METHOD (hot and cold water dyes):
1 Weigh 500g Manutex F *or* Manutex RS pre-mixed thickener into a 1 litre beaker.
2 Measure 10g Matexil P-AL and add to the Manutex, stirring thoroughly.
3 Next weigh out 50g urea and dissolve in a small amount of boiling water (for fine silk, reduce or omit if preferred). Depending on cloth and method of fixation, certain colours may benefit from increased urea quantity – always test first. Gradually add to the Manutex mixture.
4 Weigh the dye into another stainless steel jug and dissolve thoroughly in hot water.
5 Add gradually to the thickener, stirring well between each addition.

NOTE:
- If mixing turquoise, it can be beneficial to combine the dyestuff with the urea in their dry states, and then add hot water to dissolve

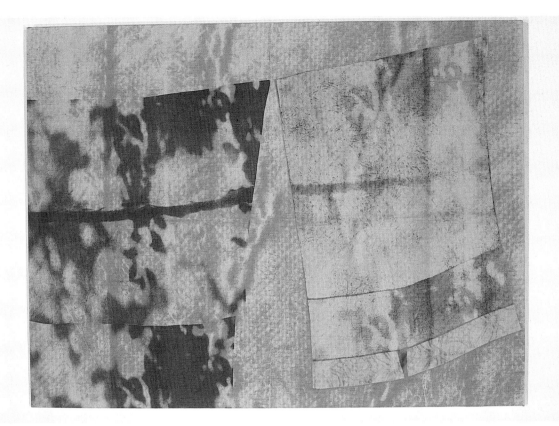

Joanna Kinnersly-Taylor (UK)
'Dream Imprint at 4pm', 2000
Dyed and screen-printed with reactive dyes and discharge on stretched linen – 113cm x 84cm x 1.7cm
in private collection – Photo: Ruth Clark

6 Weigh out 30g sodium bicarbonate and dissolve in a little hot water to form a 'slurry', and gradually add to the paste. Remember to omit this stage, if preferred, when printing on wool (see other variations on previous page).

7 Finally, assess consistency of paste and gradually add required amount of water to bring to the desired viscosity.

NOTE:

- Once the sodium bicarbonate has been added to the paste, it will keep for one month. It is possible to extend the lifespan for a further month, with the addition of a further 30g dissolved sodium bicarbonate per 1000g paste, although this is *not* feasible with all colours, e.g. turquoise and some blues; always test first. After 2 months, discard paste as both colour and consistency will have deteriorated.

Painting onto the cloth with cold water dyes
Cold water dyes in solution can also be painted directly onto the fabric. Exact quantities of dye will become apparent through experimentation, as the colour will appear darker in solution. The following is a guide only:

1 For a weak solution, dissolve 0.3g dye in 100ml hot water *or*
for a stronger solution, dissolve 1.2g dye in 100ml hot water.

2 For air-fixing, add 3g urea and 1g sodium carbonate both per 100ml water to the dye solution, stirring well *or* if steaming, omit the urea and add 3g sodium *bi*carbonate per 100ml solution, instead of the sodium carbonate.

3 Apply directly to the cloth and allow to dry, before fixing.

NOTE:

- Once sodium carbonate or bicarbonate has been added to a cold water dye solution, it will keep for up to 1 hour. After this time, it should be 're-charged' with further additions.

Painting onto the screen with cold or hot water dyes

Alternatively, a dye solution using cold or hot water dyes can be used to paint directly onto the *outside* of the screen. Once the dye is dry on the mesh, the design can be transferred to the cloth by printing with Manutex in one of two ways:

- use the dye solution as outlined previously and print with *plain* Manutex
  or
- use the dye quantities based on previous recipe, omit the other ingredients and print with a Manutex-based *print paste* (without the dye). Once the print is dry, the cloth can be fixed as appropriate.

Printing with direct dyes

for cellulose fibres, silk, wool and viscose-rayon

THICKENER: for cellulose fibres: alginate: Manutex RS (good for absorbent fabrics and simple designs) *or* gum tragacanth *or* locust bean gum. For protein fibres: locust bean gum *or* crystal gum *or* gum arabic.

AUXILIARIES: urea (for cellulose, viscose rayon and silk) *or* glycerine (for wool), acid donor (dis-

Timorous Beasties (UK)
'Force Ten' (detail, fabric by the metre)
Screen-printed with pigment dyes on linen
Photo: Alan Dimmick

odium hydrogen phosphate) (optional, hard water areas), a wetting-out agent (protein fibres), plus a fixing agent which is used in the first cold rinse at washing out.

STRENGTHS: 1–50g dye per 1000g paste.

FIXING METHODS: saturated steaming at atmospheric pressure: 45–60 minutes.

WASHING OUT: cold water with 2ml fixing agent per litre until clear / warm water (max. 40°C (104°F)) with 2ml Metapex 26 per litre for 2 minutes / cold until clear.

Direct dyes tend to be cheaper than reactives and there is a good colour range available. However, the main disadvantage of printing with direct dyes is their poor washfastness and great care needs to be taken at the washing out stages. Unfixed dye

Victoria Richards (UK)
Bags; dyed and printed with direct dyes and discharge on duchesse satin and silk velvet
Photo: Andrea Heselton

readily seeps into unprinted areas, hence the need for a fixing agent; it is also important to keep the cloth as open as possible during washing. A direct dye print paste is applied as neutral or mildly alkaline. Therefore, if you live in an area with hard water, it may be necessary to reduce the alkalinity by adding a quantity of disodium hydrogen phosphate, especially when printing on wool.

METHOD:

1 Weigh 600g of chosen premixed thickener into a 1 litre beaker.

2 Measure 20g wetting-out agent (for protein fibres) and slowly add to the thickener.

3 Next weigh 50g urea and dissolve in boiling water *or* weigh 50–70g glycerine.

4 Weigh the dye, thoroughly dissolve in boiling water (it may also be heated if necessary) and add the urea mixture *or* glycerine to the dye solution, mixing well.

5 Gradually add this mixture to the thickener, stirring well.

6 Finally, if required, dissolve up to 20g disodium hydrogen phosphate in hot water and stir into the paste.

NOTES:

- After printing, do not dry with excessive heat
- The fastness of most direct dyes will not withstand more than about 5 washes
- Many direct dyes are known to be carcinogenic

Printing with vat dyes

for cellulose (except jute) and viscose rayon

THICKENER: British gum *or* gum tragacanth *or* starch ether.

AUXILIARIES: glycerine, reducing agent (Formosul), sodium carbonate.

Dawn Dupree (UK)
'Dependant Independence', 2000
Dyed, screen-printed and painted with direct dyes on
furnishing satin stretched on wooden frames –
61cm x 61cm
Photo: FXP

STRENGTHS: 50–150g dye and 60–175g reducing agent per 1000g paste.

FIXING METHODS: (as air-free as possible) saturated steaming at atmospheric pressure: 10–25 minutes.

WASHING OUT: cold wash /cold water with 2ml hydrogen peroxide (6%) per litre water and 7.5ml acetic acid (20%) per litre water for 5 minutes / hot: 90°–100°C (194°–212°F) with 2ml Metapex 26 per litre and 0.5g sodium carbonate per litre water for 5–20 minutes / cold.

As with the dyeing process, printed vat dyes have to be reduced in order to transfer to the cloth. This happens during steaming, when the steam used should be as air-free as possible. The print is subsequently oxidised at the rinsing stage to bring out the full colour and fix the dye.

Vat dyes possess exceptional fastness properties on cellulose fibres and there are three methods of direct application: 'all-in'; 'flash-age' and 'pad-steam'. The latter are two-stage processes, and it is the first 'all-in' procedure that is described below.

NOTE:

- The use of highly soluble potassium carbonate as a substitute for sodium carbonate may produce more successful results in some circumstances.

METHOD:

1 Weigh 600g of chosen premixed thickener. Pour a small amount of the thickener into a jug and add a little water.

2 Paste dye with 50g glycerine and stir into the watered down thickener. This helps to avoid 'specky' pastes, which result in uneven prints.

3 Weigh out required quantity of Formosul and dissolve in hot water; add to (main) thickener gradually, stirring well.

4 Weigh 80–115g sodium carbonate and dis-

Jo Budd (UK)
'Corrugated Iron'
Cotton backing, overlaid with silk organza and chiffon, monoprinted with reactive dyes, and hand-sewn – 170cm x 260cm
Photo: Kate Gadsby

solve in hot water to form a 'slurry'; add to (main) thickener, mixing thoroughly.

5 Finally, add the dye mixture to the thickener, combining thoroughly.

NOTE:

• Prints should be steamed as soon as possible after printing and moderate drying. If this is not feasible, it is possible to store the printed cloth in a polythene bag in a cool, damp-free, dark place for a short time.

Printing with basic dyes

Basic dyes are scarcely used nowadays because of their very poor light and washfastness properties; they are also known to be carcinogenic.

Because there are many other options for both direct style printing and colour discharge using dyes that are safer and with superior fastness properties, recipes for basic dyes are not included in this book.

Printing with acid dyes (all types)

for jute, sisal, wool (chlorinated is best), silk, and nylon

THICKENER: locust bean gum *or* crystal gum *or* gum arabic *or* guar gum.

AUXILIARIES: urea (best for silk) *or* glycerine (best for wool), acid donor (ammonium oxalate), a wetting-out agent.

STRENGTHS: 0.5–40g (or up to 60g for nylon) dye per 1000g paste.

FIXING METHODS: saturated steaming at atmospheric pressure: 30–60 minutes depending on cloth; see notes on the next page.

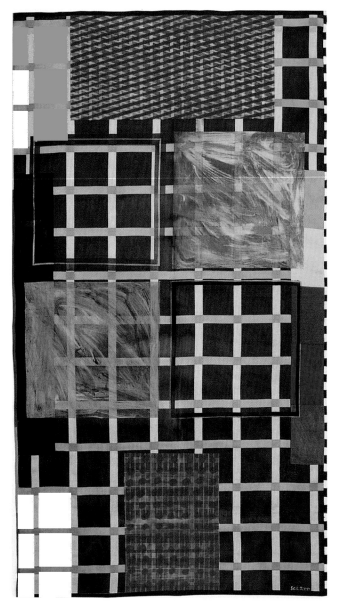

Sally Greaves-Lord (UK)
'Clamour', 2000
Hand-painted with acid dyes and discharge on silk –
91cm x 160cm
Photo: FXP

WASHING OUT: cold water until clear *or* cold water containing 1g sodium carbonate per litre until clear (nylon) / warm water (max. 40°C (104°F)) with 2ml Metapex 26 per litre for 2 minutes *with* (for nylon only) the addition of 1g sodium carbonate per litre / cold until clear.

76

NOTE:

- Whilst the use of glycerine helps reduce the adverse effects of heat during steaming on wool, it can cause bleeding on silk, and urea should be used instead

1 Measure 600g chosen premixed thickener into a 1 litre beaker.
2 Measure 20g wetting-out agent and slowly add to the thickener.
3 Next weigh either 50g urea and dissolve in boiling water *or* 50–70g glycerine.
4 Weigh the dye, thoroughly dissolve in boiling water (it may also be heated if necessary) and add the urea mixture *or* glycerine to the dye solution, mixing well.
5 Gradually add this mixture to the thickener, stirring well.
6 Finally dissolve 20g ammonium oxalate in hot water and stir into the paste.

NOTES:

- After printing, do not dry with excessive heat
- When fixing prints on nylon, steaming time is approximately 30 minutes; for other fabrics 45–60 minutes
- Acid dyes may also be used for painting directly onto the screen; see procedure under reactive dye section for application principle

Printing with disperse dyes

for cellulose acetates and tri-acetates, nylon, polyester and acrylic, also some plastics

THICKENER: alginates (Manutex F) *or* crystal gum (not suitable for high-temperature steaming) *or*

Liz Munro (UK) ▶
'Dog', 2000
Flock and puff printed and embroidered silk organza – 122cm x 244cm
Photo: Ruth Clark

Patricia Kennedy-Zafred (USA)
'Two Grandfathers'
Reactive dyed using shibori techniques and Gocco
screen-printed on cotton – 135cm x 96.5cm
Photo: Peter Shefler

locust bean gum *or* guar gum *or* British Gum – see notes on the next page.

AUXILIARIES: oxidising agent (Matexil P-AL), a wetting-out agent, plus an acid donor (disodium hydrogen phosphate) (polyester), carrier (polyester – especially with medium to deep shades), *or* urea or glycerine (cellulose acetate).

STRENGTHS: 10–100g dye per 1000g paste, depending on fabric – see notes on the next page.

FIXING METHODS: saturated steaming at atmospheric pressure: 30–45 minutes, depending on fabric or pressure steaming: 21 p.s.i. 20–30 minutes, depending on fabric; *or* baking: 200–180°C

(392°–356°F) for 30–120 seconds (polyester only) – see notes on the next page.

WASHING OUT: cold water until clear *or* (for nylon only) cold water containing 1g sodium carbonate per litre until clear / warm water (max. 40°C (104°F)) with 2ml Metapex 26 per litre for 2 minutes *with* (for nylon only) the addition of 1g sodium carbonate per litre *or* (for polyester only) hot wash at 65°–70°C (149°–158°F) with 2ml Metapex 26 per litre for 5–10 minutes *or* (for acrylic only) hot wash at 60°C (140°F) with 2ml Metapex 26 per litre for 15 minutes / cold until clear.

Disperse dyes can be used on most synthetic fabrics and are the only dyes that will colour polyester. There are variations in all aspects of production.

NOTES:

- Disperse dyes come in powder, granular and liquid form. If using the powdered dye, always sprinkle dyestuff onto water, rather than adding water to dye
- Dyes look very different in solution than the final result on cloth
- When printing on acrylic, a crystal gum such as Nafka produces the best results but should not be used for high temperature (pressure) steaming; Indalca PA/3-R is more suitable
- Although crystal gums produce prints with sharp definition, they dry to a hard film, which can crack or be difficult to remove on some fabrics during washing out. Alginates and locust bean gums are more flexible and leave no residue
- Alginate and locust bean gums must be used if prints on polyester are baked; cloth also needs to be held to width (e.g. stretched on a wooden frame) to help prevent shrinkage during baking. If printing on polyester, the addition of an acid donor (disodium hydrogen phosphate) in the print paste is necessary. If fixing by atmospheric steaming, a carrier will also be required, particularly for medium-deep shades, although colour yields are 30–50% lower than if fixed by pressure steaming
- Strengths for different fabrics:
  - cellulose acetates, tri-acetates and polyester: 10–100g dye per 1000g paste
  - polyamide (nylon) and acrylic: 30–100g dye per 1000g paste
- A guide to fixing times for different fabrics:
  - cellulose acetates: saturated steaming at atmospheric pressure: 30 minutes
  - cellulose tri–acetate: pressure steaming at 15–20 p.s.i.: 20–30 minutes

- polyamide (nylon): saturated steaming at atmospheric pressure: 30–45 minutes
- polyester: pressure steam at 21 p.s.i.: 30 minutes or bake at 200°–180°C (392°–356°F) for 30–120 seconds
- acrylic: saturated steaming at atmospheric pressure: 30–45 minutes
- Disperse dyes have best fastness properties on polyester

METHOD:

1 Weigh 500g of chosen premixed thickener into a 1 litre beaker.
2 Measure 5g Matexil P-AL and add to the thickener, stirring well.
3 Measure 20g wetting-out agent and stir into the thickener.
4 Next, if printing on polyester, weigh out 30–60g of acid donor (disodium hydrogen phosphate), dissolving it in the same weight of water, and also 3–6g carrier. Base exact quantities on colour strength of paste. Add both to the thickener mixture, stirring thoroughly.

or

if printing on cellulose acetate, weigh out 30–50g urea or glycerine (depending on strength of colour), dissolving urea in boiling water, and add slowly to the thickener mixture.

5 If using powdered or granulated dye, measure a quantity of water amounting to about 8–10 times the weight of dye and carefully sprinkle weighed dyestuff onto the surface of the water. Allow to disperse thoroughly.
6 Gradually stir dispersed dye solution or liquid dye into the thickener mixture.

Printing with pigment

Unlike other print pastes described previously, pigments do not have a natural affinity with fibres. Pigments are combined with a ready-mixed binder (see Emulsion thickeners) to form a paste that 'binds' with the fibres during fixation – mainly done by curing with heat, although most pigment discharge must be steamed – resulting in a stiffer handle than other methods. Although further treatment after curing is not needed, handle can be improved by washing the fabric very gently in warm, soapy water. Each manufacturer has their own particular pigment system, and make a variety of auxiliary products that can be used in conjunction with the range of binders to improve the type of finish, handle of the cloth, wash and rub-fastness etc. Pigment pastes are easy to mix, and keep for up to 6 months without deteriorating, providing they are kept in airtight containers in a cool place. The pigment itself is highly concentrated and has a thick, viscous consistency, making it difficult to measure accurately. Small pipettes can be used to add drops of colour gradually to the binder. Generally, screen mesh should be between 43–62T for optimum results when printing with pigment.

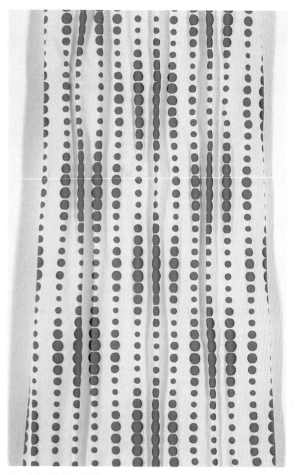

Double Helix (UK)
Fabric by the metre; puff printed cotton velvet
Photo: Ruth Clark

NOTES:

- Use non-metallic vessels to mix pigments
- If necessary, print paste can be thinned by adding 5–10g ammonium sulphate solution (diluted 1:3 with water) per litre paste, without affecting the colour strength. This also acts as a catalyst to increase the rate of curing
- If thickening is required, add up to 10g 'Printofin Supra' (Magnaprint) (or equivalent) per litre paste. This can also help to overcome problems with bleeding
- If a pastel, opaque or matt colour is required, add an opaque white binder to the standard binder. An amount of 50% opaque binder can be adequate, but with some colours a complete opaque will only be achieved with up to 70%. The resulting print may feel very stiff, depending on the coverage and fabric
- Do not exceed the maximum quantities of pigment, as the wash and rub-fastness of the print will be affected
- Curing times and temperatures given are as manufacturer's recommendations, but should be adapted as necessary to suit the base cloth and type of curer. *Always* check by sampling first
- Never use a domestic gas/electric oven to bake pigment printed fabrics, as this is a fire hazard

Natasha Kerr (UK)
'Dinner Time', 1997
Screen-printed, hand-painted and appliquéd linen
using pigment dyes – 152cm x 91cm

Pigment paste: all colours, with variation for black or white

for most natural and man-made fibres, with best handle on cellulose

THICKENER: emulsion.

AUXILIARIES: none required but various optional additions available.

STRENGTHS: 1–50g dye per 1000g paste.

FIXING METHODS: baking: 150°C (302°F) for 2–5 minutes.

WASHING OUT: not essential, but improves handle; wash gently in warm water with 2ml Metapex 26 per litre water / cold rinse to remove suds.

METHOD:

1 Weigh 999–950g pigment binder, and add between 1–50g pigment *or* if mixing black or white, weigh 999–900g pigment binder adding 1–100g pigment. Stir very thoroughly to ensure complete dispersal.

2 Print, dry and bake at 150°C (302°F) for 2–5 minutes to cure the fabric. If desired, cloth can be gently washed in warm water with 2ml Metapex 26 per litre, followed by cold rinsing to remove suds.

Pigment paste: metallic (gold, silver, bronze)

THICKENER: emulsion.

AUXILIARIES: none required, but various optional additions available.

STRENGTHS: 1–150g dye per 1000g paste.

FIXING METHODS: baking: 160°C (320°F) for 2–5 minutes.

WASHING OUT: not essential, but improves handle; wash gently in warm water with 2ml Metapex 26 per litre water / cold rinse to remove suds.

METHOD:

1 Weigh 999–850g metallic binder and gradually stir in up to 150g metallic powder, mixing thoroughly. Do not exceed this amount as proper fixation will not be possible.

2 Print and bake at 160°C (320°F) for 2–5 minutes to cure the fabric.

NOTE:

- Standard pigment colours can also be mixed with the metallic powders to achieve a variety of effects. Different binders can also be combined

Speciality binders for pigments

There are also several speciality binders available for puff, flock, pearlescent or crêpe effects. Here, sampling is paramount, as results will vary dramatically depending on base cloth, colour strength, type of curer or baker and curing temperature. For example, linen scorches very easily and it may be necessary to cure at a lower temperature for a slightly longer period. If puff prints are cured at too high a temperature, they can 'cauliflower' and then flake off; and, with flock, the surface can become very powdery. If in any doubt, begin at about 120°C (248°F) and increase temperature very gradually until the desired effect is achieved. Pigments mixed into a flock or puff binder will be much weaker than in a standard binder and so a greater quantity will be required; the final print will be 2–3 tones lighter than the colour mixed. Some printers also prefer to combine a speciality binder with a standard binder at a ratio of about 3:2 for a more subtle effect. Prints should always be cured on the same day as printing. Always refer to the

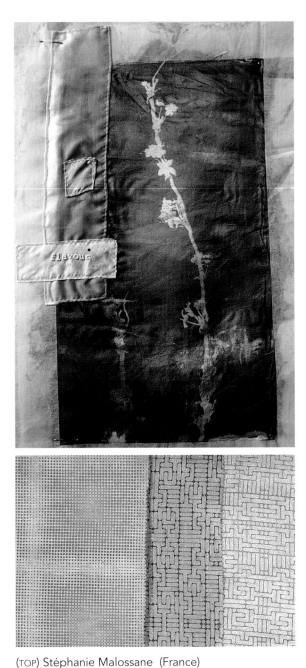

(TOP) Stéphanie Malossane (France)
'Flavour'
Puff and pigment hand-printed, hand-painted and marked Browntype on silk – 37cm x 48cm
(ABOVE) Double Helix (UK)
Fabric by the metre; metallic pigment on silk
Photo: Ruth Clark

manufacturer's instructions for optimum methods of production and experiment and adapt to meet your own specific needs.

SUMMARY OF PRINT PASTE RECIPES FOR DIRECT STYLE

Fabric	Thickener	Auxiliaries	Min/max strength of shade- per 1000g	Fixing methods and times	Washing out
Reactive: cold water	(washfastness: 5 out of 5			lightfastness: 5–6 out of 8)	
cellulose fibres, silk, viscose rayon	alginates: Manutex F or Manutex RS	urea, oxidising agent (eg. Matexil P-AL), sodium bicarbonate or a mixture of sodium bicarbonate and sodium carbonate if air fixing	0.5–50g	saturated steaming at atmospheric pressure: 10–30 mins. *or* baking 150°C (302°F): 5–10 mins. *or* air fixing	cold water until clear / hot (85–100°C (185–212°F)) + 2ml Metapex 26 per litre 5 mins. (x 2 for very deep colours) / cold until clear
wool (chlorinated is best)	alginates: Manutex F or Manutex RS	urea, oxidising agent (eg. Matexil P-AL), and, for *some colours only*, sodium bicarbonate *or* sodium carbonate (if baking); glycerine may also improve print paste	0.5–50g	saturated steaming at atmospheric pressure: 10–30 mins. *or* baking 150°C (302°F): 5–10 mins. *or* air fixing	cold water until clear / hot (85–100°C (185–212°F)) + 2ml Metapex 26 per litre 5 mins. (x 2 for very deep colours) / cold until clear
Reactive: hot water	(washfastness: 5 out of 5			lightfastness: 5–6 out of 8)	
cellulose fibres, silk, viscose rayon	alginates: Manutex F or Manutex RS	urea, oxidising agent (eg. Matexil P-AL), sodium bicarbonate *or* sodium carbonate if baking	0.5–50g	saturated steaming at atmospheric pressure: 10–30 mins. (best results) *or* baking 150°C (302°F): 5–10 mins.	cold water until clear / boil 2 mins. (except silk: not above 85°C (183°F)) + 2ml Metapex 26 per litre water / cold until clear
wool (chlorinated is best)	alginates: Manutex F or Manutex RS	urea, oxidising agent (eg. Matexil P-AL), and, for *some colours only*, sodium bicarbonate; *or* sodium carbonate (if baking); glycerine may also improve print paste	0.5–50g	saturated steaming at atmospheric pressure: 10–30 mins. (best results) or baking 150°C (302°F): 5–10 mins.	warm until clear / warm + 2ml Metapex 26 per litre 3 minutes / warm
Direct:	(washfastness: 3–4 out of 5			lightfastness: 6 out of 8)	
cellulose fibres, silk, wool and viscose rayon	cellulose: alginates: Manutex F or Manutex RS *or* gum tragacanth *or* locust bean gum protein: locust bean gum *or* crystal gum *or* gum arabic	urea (cellulose, viscose rayon and silk) *or* glycerine (wool), acid donor (disodium hydrogen phospate), wetting-out agent (protein fibres), fixing agent	1–50g	saturated steaming at atmospheric pressure: 45–60 mins.	cold + 2ml fixing agent per litre until clear / warm (max. 40°C (104°F))+ 2ml Metapex 26 per litre water 2 mins. / cold until clear

SUMMARY OF PRINT PASTE RECIPES FOR DIRECT STYLE

Fabric	Thickener	Auxiliaries	Min/max strength of shade- per 1000g	Fixing methods and times	Washing out
Vat		(washfastness: 4 out of 5		lightfastness: 6–7 out of 8)	
cellulose fibres (except jute), viscose rayon	British gum *or* gum tragacanth *or* starch ether	glycerine, reducing agent (Formosul), sodium carbonate *or* potassium carbonate	50–150g	(air-free) saturated steaming at atmospheric pressure: 10–25 minutes	cold + 2ml hydrogen peroxide (6%) and 7.5ml acetic acid (20%) per litre 5 mins. / hot (90°–100°C (194°–212°F)) + 2ml Metapex 26 and 0.5g sodium carbonate per litre water 5–20 mins. / cold
Acid (all types)		(washfastness: 4 out of 5		lightfastness: 4–5 out of 8)	
wool (chlorinated is best), silk, jute, sisal and nylon	locust bean gum *or* crystal gum *or* gum arabic *or* guar gum	urea (best for silk) *or* glycerine (best for wool), acid donor (ammonium oxalate), a wetting-out agent	0.5–40g or up to 60g for nylon	saturated steaming at atmospheric pressure: 30–60 minutes	cold until clear *or* cold + 1g sodium carbonate per litre until clear (nylon) / warm (max 40°C (104°F)) + 2ml Metapex 26 per litre water 2 mins. + (for nylon only) 1g sodium carbonate per litre / cold until clear
Disperse					
cellulose acetates and tri-acetates, nylon, polyester, acrylic and some plastics	alginates: Manutex F *or* crystal gum (not high temperature steaming) *or* locust bean gum *or* guar gum or British gum	oxidising agent (eg. Matexil P-AL), a wetting-out agent, acid donor (disodium hydrogen phosphate) (polyester), carrier (polyester) *or* urea *or* glycerine (cellulose acetate)	10–100g depending on fabrics	depends on fabric: saturated steaming at atmospheric pressure: 30–45 minutes *or* pressure steaming: 21 p.s.i. 20–30 minutes *or* baking: 200–180°C (149–158°F): 30–120 seconds (polyester only)	cold until clear *or* (for nylon only) cold + 1g sodium carbonate per litre water until clear / warm (max 40°C (104°F)) + 2ml Metapex 26 per litre water 2 mins. + (for nylon only) 1g sodium carbonate per litre water *or* (for polyester only) hot 65–70°C (149–158°F) + 2ml Metapex 26 per litre 5–10 mins. *or* (for acrylic only) hot 60°C (140°F) + 2ml Metapex 26 15 mins. / cold until clear

Fabric	Thickener	Auxiliaries	Min/max strength of shade- per 1000g	Fixing methods and times	Washing out
Pigment (all colours)					
most natural and man-made fibres, with best handle on cellulose	emulsion	none required, but various optional additions available	1–50g *or* 1–100g for black and white	baking: 150°C (302°F): 2–5 minutes depending on equipment	not essential, but improves handle; gently wash in warm water + 2ml Metapex 26 per litre / cold rinse
Pigment (metallic)					
as above	emulsion	none required, but various optional additions available	1–150g	baking: 160°C (320°F): 2–5 minutes depending on equipment	not essential, but improves handle; gently wash in warm water + 2ml Metapex 26 per litre / cold rinse

CHAPTER EIGHT

DISCHARGE

Natasha Smith (UK)
Cushions; screen-printed and stencilled silk velvet with devoré and discharge

DISCHARGE PRINTING allows, with the best set of conditions, a white or very light or bright colour to be printed on a dark background. It is a highly experimental technique, which, with practice, can achieve very striking and unusual results.

There are two types of discharge printing – 'white discharge' and 'colour discharge'. Both types of paste contain a reducing agent which removes some or all of the colour from either the dyed background or an existing print (or both), and with colour discharge, another colour, resistant to the reducing agent, is simultaneously introduced. The success of both types of discharge pastes depend upon the correct choice of dyes, thickener and auxiliaries in conjunction with the dyed base cloth or existing print. Manufacturers grade dischargeability of dyes on a scale of 1–5, with '1' having poor dischargeability and '5' being dischargeable to a good white.

WHITE DISCHARGE

A white discharge paste can be used on cloth dyed or printed with certain reactive, direct or acid dyes, and also cloth printed with pigment. Depending on the kind of effect you require, you may choose a highly dischargeable dye for your ground colour or print (to achieve a white); alternatively, a mid-graded dye, which, although will not discharge fully, will nonetheless reveal paler versions of the original colour or, sometimes, a totally different colour. When printing with a 'white' discharge paste, it is sometimes impossible to see where you have printed especially if it is of a weak strength, and the results may only become apparent after fixation.

COLOUR DISCHARGE

Dyes suitable for colour discharge are known as 'illuminating' dyes. A colour discharge paste can be made with certain reactive, direct, vat, acid and pigment dyes. If the colour discharge is of a reasonably dark shade, then the ground or print colour may not necessarily need to be highly dischargeable. Remember that for the strongest effect the illuminating dye needs to have *poor* dischargeability (i.e. be very fast), so that it withstands the effects of the reducing agent.

All discharge paste should be mixed just prior to use for best results. Ideally, do not keep longer than 24 hours (although for stronger pastes, up to 48 hours is acceptable); beyond this, the paste will lose its strength and become very runny. To avoid waste, only mix as much as you require. After printing with a discharge paste, the cloth should first be dried (avoid drying with excessive heat as the reducing agent will start to break down and not respond properly in the fixing process), and then steamed. Steaming or baking the same day is recommended for optimum results, but failing that, within 24 hours (or up to 48 hours for stronger discharge prints).

Because there are many variables in the discharge process, it is important to remember that it can be difficult to *exactly* replicate a sample on a larger scale. With all discharge techniques, testing should always be carried out first.

ASSESSING RESULTS

The factors that will define the type of results achieved when using discharge include:

- the type of dye and depth of shade used in the ground colour
- the type of dye and depth of shade used in the print (if overprinting)
- the consistency of the discharge paste in relation to the type of cloth
- the strength of the discharge paste (i.e. quantity of reducing agent)
- how fresh the discharge paste is
- the type of image being printed, i.e. fine detail or large, open areas of print, and size of screen mesh
- the number of pulls and pressure applied when printing
- thickness of cloth
- whether the existing print has been fixed or not, prior to overprinting with discharge
- how the discharge print is dried prior to fixation
- how soon after printing the cloth is steamed or baked
- how long the cloth is steamed or baked
- quality of steam

In the following recipes, three of the most common reducing agents are used:

- 'DECROLIN' (zinc formaldehyde sulphoxylate), which requires acidic conditions and is suitable for discharging on silk, wool, synthetics and with pigments on cellulose. However, going against this rule, I have also very successfully used Decrolin in a starch ether (Solivtose C5) thickener to print white discharge on reactive dyed grounds and prints on cotton and linen. Some discharge conditions cause a 'yellowing' effect, and this may be improved by the addition of zinc oxide or titanium dioxide; these ingredients also help to improve the visibility of the print before steaming.
- 'FORMOSUL' (sodium formaldehyde sulphoxylate), which needs an alkaline environment and is suitable for cellulose, viscose rayon, cellulose acetate and tri-acetate. It may also be used on silk but not on wool – it can damage and shrink the fibres. In certain situations Formosul can give a slightly 'whiter' finish than Decrolin.
- 'MANOFAST' (thiurea dioxide) is another type of reducing agent, which is less widely used now, but is useful for discharging on nylon.

So, as a *general* rule, **cellulose requires an alkaline paste**, and **protein fibres an acid paste**, although this is not hard-and-fast and it is worth experimenting. The choice of thickener and corresponding auxiliaries depend on each recipe.

◀Victoria Richards (UK)
Cope for Coventry Cathedral, 1999
Hand-painted with direct dyes and discharge on duchesse satin
Photo: Andrea Heselton

If printing on a low absorbency fabric (e.g. wool), there are various wetting-out and moisture-attracting agents that can enhance discharge penetration. However, in certain conditions, if there is an excess of these ingredients, a bleeding or 'halo' effect may occur; treating the fabric with an oxidising agent (Matexil P-AL) prior to printing may help reduce this problem. The addition of urea can help stabilise and preserve some colour discharge pastes. The minimum and maximum strengths of paste (i.e. quantity of reducing agent) also vary with each recipe. However, it should be noted that a wide range of effects can be achieved through experimenting with both very weak discharge, as well as stronger pastes; some reactive dyes, for example, will discharge very successfully with a relatively weak discharge.

IMPORTANT:
Reducing agents are harmful ingredients and must be handled with extreme care. They should be stored in air-tight containers in a dry environment, as excessive dampness can lead these ingredients to become explosive. A mask and gloves should always be worn when handling reducing agents in their dry form and subsequent mixing of discharge paste, and also on removing discharged cloth from the steamer; goggles should also be worn if fabric is heavily discharged, as fumes in the steam can hurt the eyes.

White discharge on reactive, direct and acid dyed grounds and/or prints
for cellulose, silk, wool, viscose-rayon and nylon

THICKENER: starch ether (Solvitose C5) *or* gum tragacanth (for alkaline pastes); crystal gum *or* British gum *or* guar gum *or* locust bean gum (for acid pastes).

REDUCING AGENT: Decrolin *or* Formosul (not wool) *or* Manofast (nylon).

AUXILIARIES: sodium carbonate (for cellulose fibres, optional), wetting-out agent (for wool, optional), whitener (zinc oxide or titanium oxide, optional), glycerine (nylon).

STRENGTHS: 1–200g reducing agent per 400g thickener.

FIXING METHODS: saturated steaming at atmospheric pressure: 10–30 minutes; the longer steaming times are only relevant if overprinting on previously unfixed prints.

WASHING OUT: cold water (until clear if overprinting on previously unfixed prints) / warm water (40°–50°C (104°–122°F)) with 2ml Metapex 26 per litre for 2 minutes *or* if overprinting (as above), increase hot wash to 85°–100°C (185°–212°F) / cold water (until clear).

NOTE:

- On silk, a 'halo' effect may take place. This can be improved by pre-treating the cloth in a bath made with 10ml Matexil P-AL (a mild oxidising agent) per litre water; dry before printing.

1 Weigh 400g premixed chosen thickener and gradually add any optional auxiliaries as listed above: 35g whitener; 35–65g sodium carbonate (to make a more alkaline paste, sometimes advantageous for cellulose); 15g wetting-out agent (wool); 15–35g glycerine (nylon).

2 Dissolve required amount of reducing agent in hot/boiling water (use as small a quantity of water as possible) and stir slowly and thoroughly into the thickener mixture.

NOTE:

- As with mixing print pastes, assess final viscosity of discharge and its suitability for re-

quired use and gradually add further water if necessary. For example, fine silk requires quite a thin paste in order to penetrate the fibres adequately, but should still have sufficient viscosity to avoid bleeding, which does sometimes not become apparent until after steaming

Colour discharge using reactive dyes as illuminants on reactive and direct dyed grounds and/or prints

for cellulose, silk and viscose-rayon

THICKENER: alginate thickener (Manutex F *or* Manutex RS).

REDUCING AGENT: Formosul.

AUXILIARIES: urea, sodium bicarbonate, anthraquinone powder (for a cleaner, more stable discharge, optional).

Claire O'Hea (UK)
'trilithon' cushion
Screen-printed pigment dye onto jersey lycra
46cm x 46cm
Photo: Arturo Vilar

STRENGTHS: 0.1–20g dye and 1–200g reducing agent per 500g thickener.

FIXING METHODS: saturated steaming at atmospheric pressure: 10–30 minutes.

WASHING OUT: cold water / hot (90°C (194°F)) with 2ml Metapex 26 per litre water / cold until clear.

NOTE:

1 Weigh 500g premixed chosen thickener. Dissolve 50g sodium bicarbonate in a little hot water to make a 'slurry' and add to thickener, stirring thoroughly.
2 Dissolve 10g anthraquinone powder (if required) in a little hot water and add to thickener.
3 Thoroughly dissolve 100g urea in a little boiling water, and add to thickener.
4 Weigh dye and dissolve in hot water, and gradually stir into thickener, mixing thoroughly.
5 Dissolve required amount of reducing agent in hot water and stir thoroughly into the thickener mixture.

Colour discharge using reactive, direct and acid dyes as illuminants on reactive, direct and acid dyed grounds and/or prints

for silk, wool and nylon

THICKENER: starch ether (Solvitose C5) *or* gum tragacanth (alkaline pastes) *or* British gum *or* guar gum *or* crystal gum (acid pastes).

REDUCING AGENT: Decrolin *or* Formosul (not wool) *or* Manofast (nylon).

AUXILIARIES: glycerin, a wetting-out agent (for wool, optional).

STRENGTHS: 0.1–20g dye and 1–200g reducing agent per 500g thickener.

FIXING METHODS: steaming at atmospheric pressure: 10–60 minutes (depending on dyestuff) and whether overprinting previously unfixed prints).

WASHING OUT: cold water with 2ml ammonia solution (4%) per litre / warm water (50°C (122°F)) with 2ml Metapex 26 per litre / cold.

1 Weigh 500g premixed chosen thickener and gradually add the wetting-out agent (if required).
2 Carefully mix the dye with 50g glycerin and gradually add 100–250ml hot water (based on quantity of dye). Allow to cool and then stir thoroughly into the thickener.
3 Dissolve required amount of reducing agent in hot water and stir slowly and thoroughly into the thickener mixture.

NOTE:

• The use of ammonia at the washing-out stage helps improve and retain any areas of white

Colour discharge using vat dyes as illuminants on reactive and direct dyed grounds and/or prints

for cellulose, silk and viscose-rayon

THICKENER: starch ether *or* gum tragacanth (alkaline pastes) *or* British gum *or* crystal gum (acid pastes).

REDUCING AGENT: Formosul.

AUXILIARIES: glycerine, sodium carbonate.

STRENGTHS: 1–20g dye and 20–200g reducing agent per 500g thickener.

FIXING METHODS: air-free saturated steaming at atmospheric pressure: 10–20 minutes.

WASHING OUT: cold water with 2ml hydrogen peroxide (6%) per litre and 7.5ml acetic acid (20%) per litre water for 5 minutes / hot water.

(90°–100°C (194°–212°F)) with 2ml Metapex 26 per litre and 0.5g sodium carbonate per litre water for 5 minutes / cold until clear.

METHOD:

1 Weigh 500g premixed chosen thickener. Dissolve 100g sodium bicarbonate in a little hot water to make a 'slurry' and add to thickener, stirring thoroughly.

2 Weigh the dye and carefully mix with 20g glycerine; add up to 100ml hot water (depending on dye quantity), stirring thoroughly.

3 Allow to cool and gradually add the dye solution mixture to the thickener, mixing well.

4 Dissolve required amount of reducing agent in hot water and stir slowly and thoroughly into the thickener mixture.

White and colour discharge using pigments

for use on most fabrics, but best handle on cellulose

As mentioned before, each manufacturer has their own pigment printing system, and it is important to obtain the relevant technical data sheets for the correct procedure. The processes that follow are *based on* Magnaprint's white and colour discharge systems, which use semi-emulsion acrylic binders in conjunction with both a standard reducing agent (Decrolin) and a low formaldehyde reducer. This system is one of the few that allows fixation purely by baking, should steaming facilities not be available. If this is the case, the low formaldehyde reducing agent is safer, as if the print is not washed out afterwards, there will be very little formaldehyde residue left in the cloth. However, if steaming is the preferred method of fixation, remember that if overprinting previously unfixed prints, fabric

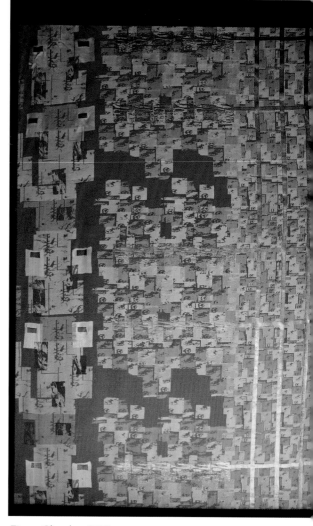

Fiona Claydon (UK)
Reactive dyed, screen-printed pigment and discharge on silk satin

should *first* be baked (to fix colour pigment) and then followed by steaming. The handle of the cloth will be improved by subsequent (very gentle) washing in warm soapy water, but this is optional. Magna recommend using 43T mesh screens (although finer mesh may be used for detailed designs) and a round profile squeegee, but this is a matter of preference.

It is worth noting that the various binders in each system can be inter-mixed. All quantities

92

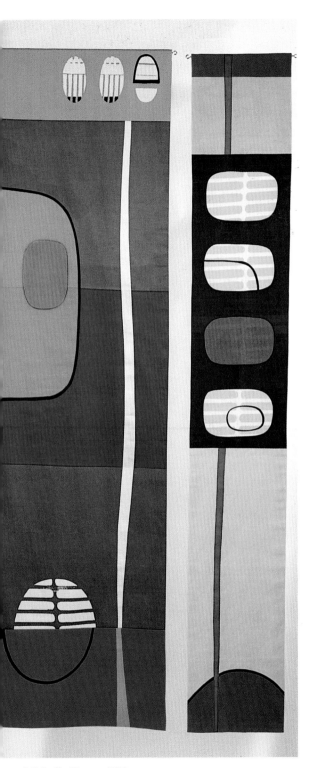

Michelle House (UK)
Untitled, 1999
Hand-painted and screen-printed with direct dyes
and pigment discharge on linen, cotton sateen and
barkweave cotton – 61cm x 216cm / 33cm x 216cm

are based on a *total* weight of 1000g of paste, so all ingredient amounts should be adjusted accordingly, retaining the ratio, if less than a litre of paste is required. The quantity of the optional 'Finish S' is *not* in addition to the 1000g paste. Once the reducing agent has been added to the paste, it should be used within 12 hours for optimum results.

Standard white discharge paste:

BINDER: Magna Discharge Super White 1400.

REDUCING AGENT: Decrolin.

AUXILIARIES: 'Finish S' (optional) to improve consistency (the binder has a high solids content).

STRENGTHS: 20–80g reducing agent per 980–920g binder.

FIXING METHOD: baking: 165°C (329°F): 4 minutes *and/or* saturated steaming at atmospheric pressure: 7–10 minutes.

WASHING OUT: (optional) gently in warm water with 2ml Metapex 26 per litre / cold rinse to remove suds.

1 Weigh 980–920g binder (incorporating up to 40g Finish S, if required). Weigh 20–80g Decrolin and sprinkle into the binder, stirring thoroughly. Allow to stand for 10 minutes prior to use.

Standard colour discharge paste:

BINDER: Magna Discharge Base A/B (for strong shades) *or* Magna Discharge Blending White 1338 (for pastel shades).

REDUCING AGENT: Decrolin.

AUXILIARIES: none required.

STRENGTHS: 1–60g pigment and 80g reducing agent per 919–860g binder.

FIXING METHOD: baking: 165°C (329°F) for 4 minutes *and/or* saturated steaming at atmospheric pressure: 7–10 minutes.

WASHING OUT: (optional) gently in warm water with 2ml Metapex 26 per litre / cold rinse to remove suds.

1 Mix as previously described, with the following variations in quantities:
  • For strong shades, use 860g, (or above), Magna Discharge Base A/B and up to 60g pigment colour, with 80g Decrolin, to make a total of 1000g
  • For pastel shades, use 915–919g Magna Discharge Blending White with up to 5g pigment colour, and 80g Decrolin to make a total of 1000g

(Low formaldehyde) white discharge paste:

BINDER: Magna Discharge Base ULF (ultra low formaldehyde).

REDUCING AGENT: Activator 'M' (in crystal form).

AUXILIARIES: none required.

STRENGTHS: 20–60g reducing agent per 980–940g binder.

FIXING METHOD: baking: 180°C (356°F) for $2^1/_2$ minutes *and/or* saturated steaming at atmospheric pressure: 7–10 minutes.

WASHING OUT: (optional) gently in warm water with 2ml Metapex 26 per litre / cold rinse to remove suds.

1 Weigh 980–940g binder and 20–60g reducing agent and sprinkle into the binder. Stir well and leave to stand for 10 minutes prior to use.

(Low formaldehyde) colour discharge paste:

BINDER: Magna Discharge Base ULF *or* Discharge Blending White ULF.

REDUCING AGENT: Activator 'M' (in crystal form).

AUXILIARIES: none required.

STRENGTHS: 1–40g pigment, and for optimum results, 60g reducing agent per 939–900g binder.

FIXING METHOD: baking: 180°C (356°F) for $2^1/_2$ minutes *and/or* saturated steaming at atmospheric pressure: 7–10 minutes.

WASHING OUT: gently in warm water with 2ml Metapex 26 per litre / cold rinse to remove suds.

1 Mix as previously described, with the following variations:
  • For strong shades, use 900g (or above) Magna Discharge Base ULF and up to 40g pigment colour and 60g Activator M to make a total of 1000g.
  • For pastel shades, use 935–939g Magna Discharge Blending White ULF with up to 5g pigment colour, and 60g Activator M to make a total of 1000g.
  • In both cases, 60g Activator M is recommended for optimum results, but it is worth experimenting with lesser quantities if working on a paler ground colour; adjust quantities of other ingredients accordingly.

SUMMARY OF PASTE RECIPES FOR DISCHARGE PRINTING

Fabric	Thickener/ binder	Reducing agent	Auxiliaries	Strengths	Fixation	Washing out
White on reactive, direct and acid grounds and/or prints						
cellulose, silk, wool, viscose rayon, nylon	starch ether *or* gum tragacanth (alkaline pastes); crystal gum *or* British gum *or* guar gum *or* locust bean gum (acid pastes)	Decrolin *or* Formosul (not wool)	sodium carbonate (cellulose, optional), wetting-out agent (wool, optional), whitener (wool, optional), glycerine (nylon)	1–200g reducing agent per 400g thickener	saturated steaming at atmospheric pressure: 10–30 minutes; (longer steaming time only relevant if overprinting on previously unfixed prints)	cold (until clear if overprinting on previously unfixed prints) / warm water 40–50°C (104–122°F) + 2ml Metapex 26 per litre 2 mins. *or* if over-printing as above, increase hot wash to 85–100°C (185–212°F) / cold until clear
Colour using reactive dyes as illuminants on reactive and direct grounds and/or prints						
cellulose, silk, viscose rayon	alginates (Manutex F *or* RS)	Decrolin *or* Formosul	urea, sodium bicarbonate, anthraquinone powder (optional)	0.1–20g dye and 1–200g reducing agent per 500g thickener.	saturated steaming at atmospheric pressure: 10–30 minutes	cold / hot 90°C (194°F) + 2ml Metapex 26 per litre / cold until clear
Colour using reactive, direct and acid dyes as illuminants on reactive, direct and acid grounds and/or prints						
silk, wool, nylon	starch ether *or* gum tragacanth (alkaline pastes); British gum *or* guar gum *or* crystal gum (acid pastes)	Decrolin *or* Formosul (not wool) *or* Manofast (nylon)	glycerine, wetting-out agent (wool, optional)	0.1–20g dye and 1–200g reducing agent per 500g thickener	saturated steaming at atmospheric pressure 10–60 minutes; (depending on dyestuff)	cold + 2ml ammonia solution (4%) per litre/ warm 50°C (122°F) + 2ml Metapex 26 per litre / cold
Colour using vat dyes as illuminants on reactive and direct grounds and/or prints						
cellulose, silk, viscose rayon	starch ether *or* gum tragacanth (alkaline pastes); British gum *or* crystal gum (acid pastes)	Formosul	glycerine, sodium carbonate	1–20g dye and 20–200g reducing agent per 500g thickener	(air-free) saturated steaming at atmospheric pressure: 10–20 minutes	cold + 2ml hydrogen peroxide (6%) per litre & 7.5ml acetic acid (20%) per litre 5 mins. / hot 90–100°C (194–212°F) + 2ml Metapex 26 per litre & 0.5g sodium carbonate per litre 5 mins. / cold until clear

SUMMARY OF PASTE RECIPES FOR DISCHARGE PRINTING

Fabric	Thickener/ binder	Reducing agent	Auxiliaries	Strengths	Fixation	Washing out
White pigment based on Magnaprint's standard white discharge paste system						
most fabrics, best handle on cellulose	Magna Discharge Superwhite 1400	Decrolin	Finish 'S' (optional)	20–80g reducing agent per 980–920g binder	baking: 165°C (329°F) 4 minutes *and/or* saturated steaming at atmospheric pressure: 7–10 minutes.	(optional) gently in warm water + 2ml Metapex 26 per litre / cold rinse to remove suds
Colour pigment based on Magnaprint's standard colour discharge paste system						
most fabrics, best handle on cellulose	Magna Discharge Base A/B (strong shades) *or* Magna Discharge Blending White 1338 (pastel shades)	Decrolin	–	1–60g pigment and 80g reducing agent per 919–860g binder	baking: 165°C (329°F) 4 minutes *and/or* saturated steaming at atmospheric pressure: 7–10 minutes.	(optional) gently in warm water + 2ml Metapex 26 per litre / cold rinse to remove suds
(Low formaldehyde) white discharge paste based on Magnaprint's ULF white discharge paste system						
most fabrics, best handle on cellulose	Magna Discharge Base ULF	Activator 'M'	–	20–60g reducing agent per 980–940g binder	baking: 180°C (356°F): 2½ minutes and/ *or* saturated steaming at atmospheric pressure: 7–10 minutes	(optional) gently in warm water + 2ml Metapex 26 per litre / cold rinse to remove suds
(Low formaldehyde) colour discharge paste based on Magnaprint's ULF white discharge paste system						
most fabrics, best handle on cellulose	Magna Discharge Base ULF or Discharge Blending White ULF	Activator 'M'	–	1–40g pigment and 60g reducing agent per 939–900g binder	baking: 180°C (356°F): 2½ minutes and/ *or* saturated steaming at atmospheric pressure: 7–10 minutes	(optional) gently in warm water + 2ml Metapex 26 per litre / cold rinse to remove suds

CHAPTER NINE

OTHER TECHNIQUES

DEVORÉ PRINTING

THIS TECHNIQUE involves printing a chemical paste, which 'burns' away one of the fibres in a mixed fibre cloth when subjected to heat. This creates patterns of open or translucent areas, contrasting with the unaffected solid fibres. The devoré paste is best applied by screen printing for maximum control and even penetration.

There are principally two types of devoré:

- an acid paste, which destroys cellulose fibres, nylon, cellulose acetate and triacetate; the active ingredient in an acid paste is either aluminium sulphate (burns away cellulose and nylon)

or

   sodium hydrogen sulphate (burns away cellulose, cellulose acetate and triacetate); this is a much more aggressive acid

and

- an alkali paste, which destroys protein fibres; the active ingredient in an alkali paste is sodium hydroxide (caustic soda)

Generally, the fibres need to be mixed in both the warp and the weft, otherwise the fabric can disintegrate. However, in a single fibre cloth, it is possible to create an interesting effect by making a complete hole, if the open areas are not too large. Other variations include:

- multi-layered: where there are two devoré-resistant fibres present
- floating thread: where the devoré-resistant fibre is only present in either the warp or the weft
- 'embossed': using a thick, single fibre fabric like cotton velvet, can, with care, result in just the pile being eaten by the devoré paste

These three-dimensional effects can be further enhanced by the use of dyeing, either before or after the devoré process:

- dyeing the polyester fibres with disperse dyes
- dyeing the cellulose fibres with reactive, direct or vat dyes
- dyeing protein fibres in acid dyes
- dyeing nylon in reactive or acid dyes
- dyeing both fibres in two different suitable dye-baths to similar shades
- dyeing both fibres in two different suitable dye-baths to contrasting shades

Coloured devoré pastes can also be used, where the colouring and devoré are undertaken in the one process:

- adding disperse dye for polyester
- adding acid dyes for nylon

Appropriate fabrics may also be first printed with an alkaline print paste (reactive, direct, vat and pigment) and subsequently overprinted with an acid devoré paste. During fixation, the alkali print neutralises the acid creating a resist. This results in unaffected solid areas of colour with the burned away areas remaining white, or as the ground colour.

NOTES:

- Reactive and pigment pastes are particularly suitable as they can be fixed by baking; direct and vat print pastes would need to be steamed first
- Care should be taken during the washing out stage if pigments are used

The reverse is also possible by first printing an acid print paste onto appropriate protein-mix fibres, which then neutralises the alkaline devoré paste during fixation. Because the fixation method with alkaline devoré is saturated steaming, the acid dye can be fixed at the same time.

As always, carry out samples first, especially to check the baking temperature.

Devoré paste

for destroying cellulose fibres, nylon, cellulose acetate and triacetate

THICKENER: locust bean gums *or* guar gum.

AUXILIARIES: glycerine (see note), urea.

Acid: aluminium sulphate (must use for nylon) *or* sodium hydrogen sulphate (must use for cellulose acetate and triacetate).

STRENGTHS: 150–250g acid per 400g thickener depending on base cloth.

NO. OF PULLS: 6–12 depending on cloth.

HEAT APPLICATION: baking: 130°–150°C (266°–284°F) for 6–12 minutes depending on equipment and base cloth *or* pressure steaming: 100 p.s.i. for 3–5 minutes.

WASHING OUT: hot water 60°C (140°F) with 2ml Metapex 26 per litre / cold / final rinse in a solution of 2gm sodium carbonate per litre water to help neutralise any remaining acid in the fibres.

Suitable fibre combinations for this recipe include: cotton-polyester, cotton-silk, viscose-polyester, viscose-silk velvet and viscose-silk satin, where the cellulose fibres will be destroyed

NOTE:

- Some printers prefer to omit the glycerine from the paste. As it is a hygroscopic agent, it

◀ Carole Waller (UK)
Oasis; 2000
Hand-painted resist, devoré printed and painted with reactive dyes on silk/viscose organza
Photo: Maggie Lambert

DEVORÉ: ASSESSING RESULTS

The following are all key factors in a successful devoré print:

- type of base cloth – fibre combination
- consistency, strength and freshness of paste
- number of pulls and pressure applied when screen-printing
- whether printing on front or back of cloth (remember to reverse design on screen if necessary)
- how print is dried
- temperature and length of time of baking
- whether the base cloth has been pre-dyed (commercially) – for example, black silk-viscose velvet may have undergone a finishing treatment making it less easy to devoré

NOTES:

- The correct number of pulls for optimum results will become apparent through sampling. As a guide, silk-viscose satin needs about 8 pulls and silk-viscose velvet 12 (on the reverse). If you do not achieve a devoré that rubs out correctly, it may be that the consistency of the paste is incorrect, rather than not having done enough pulls. An excessive number of pulls will result in bleeding and loss of sharpness of image, whilst not necessarily making fibre removal easier. Alternatively, the amount of acid may need increasing
- Some printers prefer to omit the glycerine from the paste. As it is a hygroscopic agent, it may hamper devoré quality with some finer fabrics, making it difficult to wash out burnt fibres properly. However, it can be advantageous with pile fabrics such as velvet
- It is best to print and bake cloth on the same day if possible
- Ensure the print is completely dry before baking. Sometimes it may be necessary to 're-dry' the cloth immediately prior to baking, as moisture can be absorbed from the atmosphere, making the process less effective (i.e. if printed last thing and left overnight); do this with moderate heat
- A higher baking temperature is necessary when devoré is used in conjunction with disperse dyes
- Pressure steaming is particularly effective with sodium hydrogen sulphate pastes, but the specialist equipment needed to reach the very high temperatures required are unlikely to be available in a studio situation for work on a large scale
- Pressure steaming may also be used for alkaline pastes on wool and silk, if preferred, but saturated steaming at atmospheric pressure works very well
- After baking, the printed area should have turned a pale to medium brown. If the fibres have turned dark brown to black, degradation of fibres may have proceeded too far and the remaining fibres may be stained
- Burnt fibres are removed by hand washing in hot, soapy water; place a 'spatter guard' (used for frying) over the plughole to prevent fibres from blocking up the drain. Although machine washing may give better results, the loose fibres (particularly with a pile fabric) can cause damage to the machine. Rubbing out fibres by hand *before* washing is not to be recommended, although this could be done with a small piece of cloth contained in a plastic bag; once the fibres become airborne they are a health hazard. However, any remaining fibres not removed by washing may be carefully taken out by hand – a hand-held vacuum cleaner can be a useful aid, but always wear a mask, goggles and gloves
- The aluminium sulphate in acid pastes to be iron-free. Although an uncommon occurrence, if there is an impurity in the crystals, it will combine with other elements in the thickener, re-forming into a new compound, resulting in an unsatisfactory print

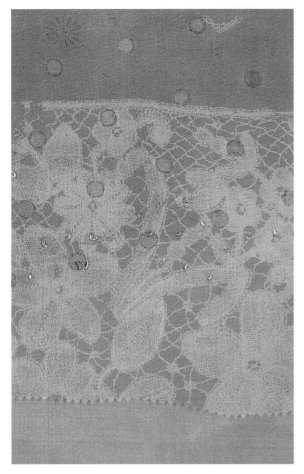

Flora Roberts (UK)
Screen-printed discharge and devoré on cotton and cotton organza.
Photo: Ruth Clark

may hamper devoré quality with some fabrics, making it difficult to wash out burnt fibres properly.

METHOD:

1 Weigh 400g of your chosen premixed thickener.

2 Dissolve up to 10g urea in boiling water and add to thickener with 80g glycerine, stirring thoroughly. The glycerine acts as a drying retardant, allowing the paste to properly penetrate into the cloth (especially with pile fabrics).

3 Weigh 150–250g (depending on base cloth) aluminium sulphate *or* sodium hydrogen sulphate and mix in enough hot water to dissolve thoroughly. Gradually stir into the thickener mixture and add more water, as required, to reach the desired consistency, which ideally should be glossy and thick, but easily poured. Leave to stand for 2 hours.

4 Print and allow to dry naturally, if possible. Bake or steam at the required temperature until the cellulose has turned light to medium brown in shade. If printing small areas, an iron may be used with care, providing the unprinted cloth is not scorched. However, it is always best to carry out samples in the same manner as the final piece.

5 Wash out burnt fibres as outlined in the notes and if desired, use sodium carbonate in the final rinse to help neutralise any remaining acid in the fibres.

Coloured devoré paste with disperse dye

for colouring polyester and destroying cellulose fibres, nylon, cellulose acetate and triacetate

THICKENER: locust bean gums *or* guar gum.

AUXILIARIES: glycerine, polyester carrier.

ACID: aluminium sulphate (must use for nylon) *or* sodium hydrogen sulphate (must use for cellulose acetate and triacetate).

STRENGTHS: 150–250g acid per 400g thickener depending on base cloth / 4–40g disperse dye per 400g thickener.

NO. OF PULLS: 6–12 depending on cloth.

HEAT APPLICATION/FIXATION: baking: 200–180°C (392°–356°F) for 30–120 seconds depending on equipment and base cloth *or* pressure steam: 100 p.s.i: 3–5 minutes.

WASHING OUT: hot water 65–70°C (149–158°F) with 2ml Metapex 26 per litre 5–10 minutes to clear excess disperse dye / cold / final rinse in a solution of 2gm sodium carbonate per litre water to help neutralise any remaining acid in the fibres.

By incorporating disperse dye to the devoré paste, the colouring of the polyester fibres in the fabric and the burning away of cellulose can be undertaken in one process. The unprinted cellulose areas will remain white. As the disperse dye is fixed and the devoré baked simultaneously, a higher temperature will be required.

METHOD:

1 Weigh 400g of your chosen premixed thickener and stir in 80g glycerine.
2 If using powdered dye, measure a quantity of water amounting to about 8 times its weight and carefully sprinkle dyestuff onto the surface of the water. Allow to disperse thoroughly.
3 Measure 15g polyester carrier and stir into dye solution.
4 Gradually add the dye solution into the thickener, stirring thoroughly.
5 Weigh 150–250g (depending on base cloth) aluminium sulphate or sodium hydrogen sulphate and mix in enough hot water to dissolve thoroughly. Gradually stir into the thickener mixture and add more water, as required, to reach the desired consistency, as Step 2 in the previous recipe. Leave to stand for 2 hours.
6 Print and dry as before. Fix and wash out as described.

Devoré paste

for destroying protein fibres

THICKENER: starch ether (Solvitose C5).

AUXILIARIES: none required.

ALKALI: sodium hydroxide solution 48° Bé (100° Tw).

STRENGTHS: 250g alkali per 400g thickener.

NO. OF PULLS: 6–10 depending on cloth.

HEAT APPLICATION: saturated steam at atmospheric pressure: 30+ minutes *or* pressure steam at 10 p.s.i.: 10 minutes.

WASHING OUT: rinse in a bath containing 2ml acetic acid (20%) per litre water to neutralise the alkali / cold.

Suitable fibre combinations for this recipe include: silk-polyester, silk-metal, wool-cellulose, wool-polyester and wool-acrylic, where the protein fibres will be destroyed.

This devoré paste requires the sodium hydroxide solution to be at a specific gravity or viscosity and this is measured with a hydrometer using the Baumé (° Bé) or Twaddell (° Tw) scales.

METHOD:

1 Weigh 400g of premixed thickener.
2 Gradually stir in 250g sodium hydroxide solution 48° Bé (100° Tw) and add enough water to achieve the desired consistency.
3 Print and allow to dry naturally (see notes).
4 Steam to fix; the protein fibres will turn yellow-orange in colour.
5 Wash out as described.

NOTES:

- Handle the devoré paste with great care as caustic solutions will burn
- If printing on a wool mix knitted fabric, it can be necessary to felt the cloth before printing, to help prevent broken wool threads unravelling. Do this by washing in hot, soapy water followed by cold rinsing

LEFT Caroline Bartlett (UK)
'Encoded', 2000; sited at 6 Brindley Place,
The Waterfront, Birmingham;
architects Allies and Morrison for Argent plc;
commissioned through Contemporary Applied Arts
Reactive dyed, pigment printed and pleated linen
190cm x 500cm

ABOVE 'Encoded' (detail),
Photos: Pete Massingham

103

CRIMPING

In the mercerisation process, bleached cotton is saturated with a strong, alkaline caustic soda solution, causing the fibres to contract and swell, which results in a stronger, more lustrous fabric which has a greater affinity for dyestuffs. By applying a crimping paste to cotton by hand or through screen-printing, localised mercerisation will take place, causing untreated areas to shrink and pucker, imitating the qualities and effect of a woven seersucker fabric. Cotton poplin is the most suitable cloth for this process.

The crimping procedure is potentially hazardous and great care should be taken when working with strong, caustic solutions. Wear gloves, goggles and suitable clothing, to protect against serious burns. If stainless steel containers are used for part of the mixing process, they must be washed thoroughly after use; do not use aluminium vessels.

If applying the paste through a screen, wash immediately after printing, as the strong solution can destroy the screen coating. If hand-painting, use brushes with synthetic bristles only. Pin the cotton fabric into a thick backing cloth on the print table, but do not over-tension. After applying the paste, the pins should be removed, to allow the fabric to contract without restriction. Wash table as soon as cloth is removed.

Fabric may be dyed with reactive dyes before or after the crimping process but bear in mind that crimped areas will appear darker. A coloured crimping paste may also be used by adding an alkali-resistant dyestuff – reactive, direct or vat are all suitable.

Plain crimping paste

for bleached (unmercerised) cotton

THICKENER: starch ether (Solivitose C5) *or* crystal gum

ALKALI: sodium hydroxide solution 48° Bé (100° Tw)

AUXILIARIES: none

NO. OF PULLS: 2–4 depending on cloth

WASHING OUT: cold water (removing all alkali) / cold water with 2ml acetic acid (20%) per litre / hot water / cold water

METHOD

1 Weigh 360g chosen premixed thickener and gradually and thoroughly stir in 640g sodium hydroxide solution as described. If necessary, a little water may be added to achieve desired consistency.

2 Print, unpin cloth and leave to contract for up to 1 hour.

Patricia Black (Australia)
'Scorched',
Shibori processes: clamped resist, discharge, overdyed and pole-wrapping
('arashi') on silk organza
Photo: Dean Turkot

Coloured crimping paste

for bleached (unmercerised) cotton

THICKENER: crystal gum (Nafka – direct dyes) *or* alginate (Manutex F or RS – reactive dyes) *or* starch ether (Solvitose C5) *or* gum tragacanth (vat dyes).

ALKALI: sodium hydroxide solution 48° Bé (100° Tw).

DYESTUFF: reactive, direct *or* vat.

AUXILIARIES: urea (for reactive dyes) *or* glycerine *and* reducing agent (Formosul) (for vat dyes).

NO. OF PULLS: 2–4 depending on cloth.

FIXING METHOD: steaming at atmospheric pressure: 10–45 minutes (depending on dyestuff).

WASHING OUT: cold water (removing all alkali) / cold water with 2ml acetic acid (20%) per litre / hot water / cold water taking care to remove all excess dye.

METHOD:

To mix approximately 1000g coloured crimping paste:

1 Weigh 360g chosen premixed thickener and gradually and thoroughly, stir in 640g sodium hydroxide solution as described.

2 For reactive dyes, dissolve 100g urea in boiling water *or* for vat dyes weigh 50–100g Formosul (dissolved in hot water), and stir into thickening.

3 Dissolve 25g chosen dyestuff in hot water; for vat dyes, paste first with 20g glycerine and then add water, stirring thoroughly. Add dye solution to thickening, mixing well.

4 Print and allow to dry as before. After steaming, allow cloth to sit for a few minutes before washing out.

Joanna Kinnersly-Taylor (UK)
'Memory Imprint in Green' (detail), 1998
Dyed, screen-printed and hand-painted on linen
using reactive dyes and discharge; 36cm x 180cm
In private collection
Photo: Ruth Clark

SUMMARY OF PASTE RECIPES FOR DEVORÉ PRINTING AND CRIMPING

Suitable fibre combinations	Thickener	Auxiliaries	Strengths	No of pulls	Heat application/ fixation	Washing out
Devoré: acid: aluminium sulphate or sodium hydrogen sulphate						
cotton-polyester, cotton-silk, viscose-polyester, viscose-silk velvet, viscose-silk satin, also nylon mixes (aluminium sulphate only) and cellulose acetate and triacetate (sodium hydrogen sulphate only)	locust bean gums *or* guar gum	glycerine, urea	150–250g per 400g thickener	6–12	baking: 130–150°C (266–284°F): 6–12 minutes, depending on equipment and base cloth; *or* pressure steaming: 100 p.s.i. 3–5 minutes	hot water 60°C (140°F) + 2ml Metapex 26 per litre water / cold / final rinse in cold + 2g sodium carbonate per litre water to neutralise any remaining acid
Devoré: coloured acid: aluminium sulphate or sodium hydrogen sulphate with disperse dye						
cotton-polyester, viscose-polyester	locust bean gums *or* guar gum	glycerine, carrier	150–250g with 10–100g dye per 400g thickener	6–12	baking: 200–180°C (392–356°F): 30–120 seconds, as above; *or* pressure steaming: 100 p.s.i. 3–5 minutes	hot water 65–70°C (149–158°F) + 2ml Metapex 26 per litre water 5–10 mins. / cold / final rinse in cold + 2g sodium carbonate per litre to neutralise any remaining acid
Devoré: alkali: sodium hydroxide						
silk-polyester, silk-metal, wool-cellulose, wool-polyester, wool-acrylic	starch ether	–	250g per 400g thickener	6–10	saturated steam at atmospheric pressure: 30+ minutes; *or* pressure steam at 10 p.s.i.: 10 minutes	cold + 2ml acetic acid (20%) per litre water / cold
Crimping: alkali plain						
bleached (un-mercerised) cotton	starch ether *or* crystal gum	–	640g per 360g thickener	2–4	leave for up to 1 hour	cold to remove all alkali/ cold + 2ml acetic acid (20%) per litre / hot / cold
Crimping: alkali coloured: with reactive, direct or vat dyes						
bleached (unmercerised) cotton	crystal gum (Nafka – direct) *or* alginate (Manutex F *or* RS – reactive) or starch ether *or* gum tragacanth (vat)	urea, (reactives) or glycerine and reducing agent (Formosul) (vat)	640g with 25g dye per 360g thickener	2–4	leave for up to 1 hour then saturated steaming at atmospheric pressure: 10–60 minutes (depending on dyestuff)	leave for a few minutes after steaming then cold to remove all alkali/ cold + 2ml acetic acid (20%) per litre / hot / cold

By using a special adhesive, either through screen-printing or hand-painting, metallic foils can be applied to fabric by heat and pressure to achieve a reflective surface. There is no limitation to the intricacy of design, providing the glue is of a printable consistency. Foils are available by the roll in a variety of finishes and widths; it can be overlapped if necessary in order to cover large areas. Spirit-based adhesives like 'Metatran' (Sericol), are specifically designed for foil application and can be diluted with white spirit to reach the desired consistency. The drawback of a solvent-based glue is cleaning the screen after printing. A soluble screen wash (i.e. one that mixes with water) is gently applied to the screen and left for up to 1 minute, **but no longer**, otherwise the image will start to break down; the screen is then hosed down in the normal way. An alternative is to use a water-based adhesive specifically designed for flock (see opposite). 'Flock Transfer FT' (also Sericol) has proved to be particularly effective as a glue for foil application, can be watered down, and is naturally much easier to clean off the screen. A heat press is the preferred method of applying heat as an even amount of pressure will be achieved, although it may be possible to produce successful foil finishes using an iron, depending on the size of design and type of fabric. The exact temperature will depend on the equipment used.

The factors that should be taken into account when using foils include:

- type of base cloth
- consistency of the adhesive in relation to the screen mesh size and detail of design
- number of pulls
- length of time left to dry and in what conditions
- temperature of heat press or iron
- pressure applied during heat treatment

METHOD:

1 Screen-print design onto cloth using chosen adhesive.
2 Depending on manufacturer's instructions, leave to dry thoroughly for the required length of time.
3 Cut foil a little bigger than the size of the printed design and lay onto the cloth *shiny or patterned side up.*

4 Set the heat press to 165–170°C (329–338°F) and at the correct pressure, and place cloth and foil (cloth side down) between the protective silicone sheets. Set for 20 seconds.
5 Allow to cool before carefully peeling off the backing paper; the foil should then have transferred successfully to the glue-printed design.

You will then have a negative version of the design left on the foil and this can be utilised if desired:

1 Cut a piece of Bondaweb to the correct size and place glue side down, onto a piece of cloth.
2 Set with heat under the heat press, time and temperature as before, and once cool, peel off backing paper.
3 Then lay the negative foil sheet (shiny side up) over the Bondaweb surface and place under the heat press as before.
4 Peel away the foil backing sheet and it will

be completely clear, the negative foil image now having transferred to the Bondaweb surface.

5 Finally, a foil of a different colour may be used to fill the positive (Bondaweb) shapes that are left.

FLOCKING

This is a different effect to that achieved in pigment printing with a speciality flocking binder, as here the flock comes in the form of flocking paper. First a special adhesive such as 'Flock Transfer FT' (Sericol) is screen-printed/hand-painted onto the base cloth with the flocking paper subsequently transferred though heat and pressure. This results in a completely smooth, fine flocked surface, without distorting the fabric. As with foil, there is no limitation to the fineness of design.

Flocking paper can be purchased on rolls 50cm wide; larger sizes are available but they tend to be expensive. It is produced in a limited colour range, including black and white, but can be dyed gently in a reactive or direct dye-bath. To avoid damaging the backing paper, the viscose rayon flock should be dyed in as large a vessel as possible with minimum agitation. Experimentation is required to ascertain which dye-bath is best for the colour required. Although a reactive dye-bath will not expose the flock to excessive heat (which can cause the paper to disintegrate), the length of time needed to achieve a full shade may be excessive. A direct dye-bath may be more appropriate, as despite the higher temperature, the flock could be removed as soon as the desired colour is reached.

Flock printed fabrics may be washed gently in temperatures from 40°– 60°C (104°–140°F), *two to three days* after application, by which time the flock will have fully adhered to the fabric. This means that subsequent processes may then be carried out, for example, overprinting, discharge, further dyeing etc. Flock printed cloth is also suitable for dry-cleaning.

The principal of application and factors to be considered are very similar to that of foil described above.

METHOD:

1 Screen-print or hand-paint a suitable flocking adhesive such as Flock Transfer FT onto fabric.
2 Depending on manufacturer's instructions, leave to dry thoroughly for the required length of time. With Sericol's Flock Transfer FT, this means air-drying for 1–1$\frac{1}{2}$ hours, or force drying in baker at 100°–110°C (212°–230°F) for 3–5 minutes.
3 Cut flocking paper a little bigger than the size of the printed design and lay onto the cloth *flock side down.*
4 Set the heat press to 165°–170°C (329°–338°F) and at the correct pressure, and place cloth and flock (cloth side down) between the protective silicone sheets. Set for 20 seconds.
5 Allow to cool before carefully peeling off the backing paper; the flock should then have transferred successfully to the glue-printed design.

The remaining negative flock shapes may be utilised as described for foils above.

A resist paste forms a barrier, preventing penetration of dye or print paste into the 'resisted' areas. There are many types of resist pastes made from gums, waxes, resins and starches that are suitable for a wide range of fabrics, techniques and effects. These can be applied directly onto the cloth using a variety of tools, or painted directly onto the screen mesh. A starch-based paste is one of the simplest to make and is suitable for painting over with print paste or dyes; it can then be subjected to steam to enable the dyes to be fixed. Depending on the fabric and thickness of paste, the starch resist will shrink and crack when dye is applied, producing a range of patterns. Potato and corn dextrin are particularly suitable for this, and do not permanently shrink the fabric. Potato starch forms a stable medium when mixed with water and is a versatile resist or anti-fusant for water-based dyes. After washing out, there is no starch residue and so the handle of the cloth remains unaffected.

Just three resist pastes are described here.

Flour paste:

plain flour, alum (potassium aluminium sulphate) and water.

NOTES:

- alum can be bought from a chemist and may come in either powder or crystal form. If crystals are used, boiling water will need to be added and the mixture left for a while to break down
- results of this technique will depend very much on consistency of paste, thickness to which it is applied, type of cloth used, ambient temperature etc.; as ever, testing is the key to success

1 Weigh 112g plain white flour into a bowl and add 4g alum powder or dissolved crystal solu-

Mary Ann Chatterton (UK) ▶
Detail of flour paste resist and hand-painted reactive dyes on silk jersey
For Nana Agyeman's Autumn 2000 Collection
Photo: Ruth Clark

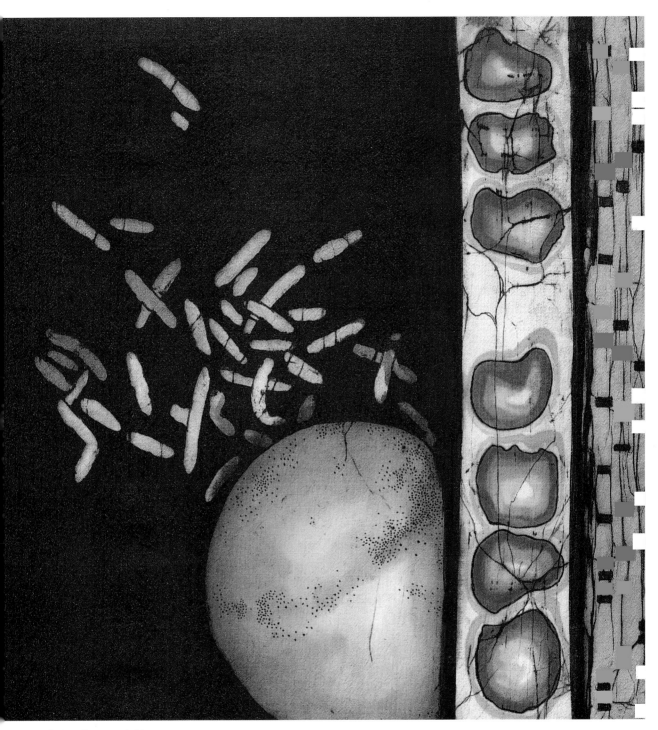

Sarah Stephenson (UK)
'Genetics, prompting questions for the future', 2000
Japanese wax resist (*roketsu-zome*), hand-painted and
dyed with reactive cold water dyes and *Kniazeff* silk
paints on Thai silk taffeta – 30cm x 30cm
Photo: Richard Dawson

tion. Add water gradually to produce an elastic consistency that is thick enough to coat the
back of a spoon.

2   Pin out cloth onto a thick backing cloth, but
do not over stretch. Apply paste to cloth with

a brush, to a depth of up to about ¼ in. thick. To create fine lines, paste can be squeezed out through a plastic bottle with a nozzle.

3 Leave paste to dry thoroughly until the surface is hard; cloth can be pulled at each end to encourage cracking of the surface. Print paste can then be painted over the paste and will colour the cloth through the cracks. By distorting the cloth *before* the paste is dry, larger sections of paste will fall off, enabling different texture to be achieved.

4 After steaming, the paste must be removed by washing in a bucket of hot water; a nail brush will aid this process. Alternatively, if washing out a larger piece of fabric, it could be taped on a shower wall and washed down using a scrubbing brush. Do not tip flour paste residue straight down the drain, as it will cause blockages; filter through a sieve or spatter guard (used over a frying pan).

5 Then wash the cloth thoroughly in hot soapy water, before a final cold rinse.

Flour and gum arabic paste

A flour-based paste mixed with gum arabic will make a more flexible resist suitable for screen-printing, as well as painting or block printing.

1 In a heat-proof vessel, mix 100g plain flour with 100ml cold water and, stirring continuously, heat until thick.

2 Allow to cool a little, before slowly mixing in 100g premixed gum arabic solution (see recipe in Chapter 6). Add a little water if necessary to reach desired consistency.

Manutex F gum resist

Manutex F gum can be used to paint directly onto the screen to block off unwanted areas. Allow to dry thoroughly before printing as normal. Many consecutive prints will be possible if printing with dyes, but pigment breaks down the Manutex more quickly. The Manutex can be applied through a paper stencil for a more defined shape. Wash screen off thoroughly, ensuring no mesh is blocked.

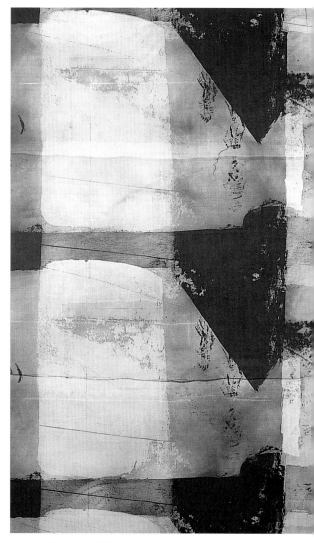

Lynne Gibbons (UK)
Detail from 3m length, 2000
Screen-printed with reactive dyes and discharge, incorporating Manutex resist, on ribbed cotton
Photo: Ruth Clark

Transfer or sublimation printing is a technique developed for use on synthetics (polyester is best) or mixed fibre cloth with a high synthetic content. Disperse dyes are applied to non-absorbent paper, which, in the presence of heat and pressure, vapourise and condense onto the surface of the fabric.

Disperse dyes and pastes, inks and special transfer crayons and pencils can be applied to a variety of papers that allow the heat to penetrate. A lightweight cartridge or recycled paper gives the best colour yield, with watercolour paper transferring texture but giving a much paler shade. Paper should be stretched or taped down to prevent buckling, with colour being applied in several washes to ensure even transference to cloth. If using a disperse dye paste, the gum acts as a resist, creating slight texture and a 'ghostly' outline print. Alternatively, specialist pre-dyed papers can be bought.

With all media, sampling is necessary, as the inks look dull on the paper, with colour often changing dramatically after application. The quantity of dye will depend on the colour; approximately 10g dye/200ml water will cover 2–3 sheets of A2 paper. Ensure that dye is thoroughly dissolved to avoid specks of dye appearing on the print.

An iron or heat press can be used to transfer the design. The cloth, with transfer paper placed face down on top, should be sandwiched between two layers of silicon-coated paper (or other thin paper if using an iron), to protect the surface of the table, iron or heat press and stop the fabric from scorching. An iron should be used on its hottest setting until dye transferral is complete, with a heat press

Julie Anne Hughes (UK)
Heat transfer print with disperse dyes on polyester satin

Wendy Edmonds (UK)
Cushions - mesh and leaf (detail)
Heat transfer print with disperse dye on matt satin polyester
Photo: Nick Turner

set at between 180°–200°C (356°–392°F) for about 20–30 seconds, although care should be taken with certain organza-type fabrics which may bubble up or melt. If colour is always applied quite heavily to the paper, a wide range of shades can be achieved by experimenting with the length of time the cloth is held under the heat press, this could be from as little as 2 to 60 seconds.

Different effects can also be achieved by printing on textured cloth and knits. Heat 'photograms' are possible by using flat objects such as leaves, feathers, lace, open weave fabrics, thread etc. as a mask, to create silhouettes. A 'halo' effect will be created with 'thicker' items, but care should be taken not to damage the heat press; flat metal objects, for example, can dent the plates which become 'soft' to metals when very hot. After heat application, dyes are fixed; if paste was used, the cloth should then be washed off as for disperse prints.

ALTERNATIVE PHOTOGRAPHIC PROCESSES

There are several historic photographic printing processes which can be applied *directly to cloth* and these include cyanotype or blueprint and Van Dyke prints. For further information on traditional techniques, see these two excellent web sites:
www.cyanotypes.com and www.mikeware.demon.co.uk

Carol Adleman (USA)
'Gone' (detail), 1995
Cyanotype on cotton netting, found photo collage – 58.5cm x 46cm
Photo: Dan Kahler

DIGITAL PRINTING

Digital printing uses the most up-to-date technology to produce printed cloth without the need for screens. Designs can be created by scanning and manipulating imagery in a software programme such as 'Adobe Photoshop', and printed fabric can be generated directly from the computer disc via the digital printer, in a very similar way as one would print onto paper with an inkjet printer.

This new technology is appealing to large manufacturers who can produce samples of new ranges, with the potential for customisation, without major investment. Digital printing also allows industry to respond quickly to new and changing markets. For the small-scale textile printer, digital printing allows experimentation, innovation and production of small-medium print runs; most large printers have a 500m minimum order.

TOP The 'Amethyst' bulk production digital printer ▲ and ABOVE (pressurised) steamer at the Centre for Advanced Textiles, Glasgow School of Art

◀ Kate Woods (UK)
Digital print on silk viscose satin using 'drop on demand' (DOD) technology – 50cm x 135cm

Different printers can be set up to use one of a variety of dye types (e.g. reactive or disperse) and these inks come in liquid form with a shelf life of 1–2 years. Cloth has to be pre-treated prior to printing. For example, if using reactive dyes, a sodium bicarbonate solution would be applied to allow subsequent fixation and washing, and this can be carried out on a small scale in the studio. However, fabric suppliers are increasingly offering pre-treated fabrics, though there are still some problems associated with ensuring a completely even coating and this does not become apparent until after steaming and washing out. Pre-treated cloth should be stored away from direct sunlight and also has a lifespan of 1–2 years. After steaming, prints. are quickly washed off in the normal way, as there is minimal excess dye to clear. Because of this, and the fact that there are no screen processing re-

Kendra McCallum (UK)
'The Motion Collection', 2000
Digitally printed on crêpe silk using the Stork
'Amethyst' – 158 cm x 130cm
Photo: Ruth Clark

lated chemicals, there is virtually no effluence created, making digital printing ecologically superior to traditional methods.

There are three digital printing technologies currently in use.

CONTINUOUS STREAM

This technology has been developed by the Dutch company Stork. The True Colour Printer (TCP) and the 'Amethyst' Bulk Production Printer use the so-called 'Hertz' principle, where electrically charged vibrations split up the inkjet into very small droplets at a rate of 625,000 per second, with a magnetic field removing unwanted droplets. This 'continuous stream' print-head technology produces up to 16 droplets of dye on the same pixel, allowing smooth continuous tones and a very high quality of detail and colour reliability.

Glasgow School of Art's Centre for Advanced Textiles uses both these printers. The 'Amethyst', the world's first bulk production printer, is capable of printing 18m^2 per hour and can be left unattended for 16 hours allowing overnight printing. The True Colour Printer has a 1m^2 per hour production capability, making it more suited to printing strike-off 'coupons'; its print quality is superior to that of the Amethyst.

Using these printers, photographic quality imaging for printed textiles is achievable. There is no colour limit and a wide range of fabrics from velvets to sheers can be printed with reactive dyes, allowing tremendous scope for innovation. It is also possible to print a repeat unit of up to 5m (16ft) in length. GSA's Amethyst fixation unit uses air-free pressurised steaming and has a capacity of about 60 metres of cloth per hour.

At the time of writing GSA was thought to be the only educational institution in the world to have these digital printing facilities. It also runs a Bureau service actively supporting small UK textile businesses as well as catering for the global market.

DROP ON DEMAND (DOD)

Developed by Mimaki in Japan, these are currently widely used in the UK. Using piezo head technology, ink is delivered using an electric charge through quartz crystals. It is a 4 or 8 colour process and it is possible to use a range of dyes. Printing at 720 dpi ensures good colour saturation, but only produces 2–3m^2 per hour, requiring constant supervision.

THERMAL BUBBLEJET TECHNOLOGY

This process is being superseded by continuous stream and DOD technologies. Ink is forced through the print-head by a temperature increase. It uses a 4 colour process, with a lower 330 dpi and 600 dpi resulting in poor colour saturation. Pigment cannot be used with this system.

CHAPTER TEN

PREPARING IMAGERY AND SCREENS FOR PRINTING

Examples of different methods and materials for translating artwork

METHODS OF TRANSFERRING IMAGERY TO A SCREEN

STENCILS

Paper Stencils

Stencils can be cut from newsprint, for a one-off print, or thicker paper for several prints in succession. For a stencil or mask that is needed long-term, thick acetate film or drafting film, such as Kodatrace, is very useful, as it can be hosed down and re-used without buckling or distorting. Stencils or masks can either be stuck to the cloth with small pieces of masking tape or attached directly to the screen.

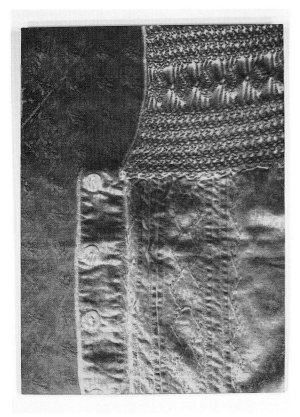

Joanna Kinnersly-Taylor (UK)
'Lattice Plain', 2000
Dyed and screen-printed with reactive dyes and discharge on stretched linen – 84cm x 113cm x 1.7cm
Photo: Ruth Clark

Plastic film stencils

This film makes a more hard-wearing stencil and is ideal for creating designs which have flat or large areas of colour; intricate designs are also possible. Areas of the design that are required to print are cut away using a sharp scalpel, initially through the film layer only, leaving the acetate backing in tact. The stencil is then adhered to the screen using heat or an adhering fluid, with the backing being peeled away, and is durable enough for repeated printing. Brand names include 'Autotype Solvent Green' (Sericol) and 'Profilm' (Selectasine).

PHOTOGRAPHIC STENCILS

An image transferred to a screen photographically will be hard-wearing and allows a huge variety of texture and opacity to be translated onto cloth. A 'film positive' is the name given to the film onto which the design has been reproduced (using one of the methods described below) and which is ready for exposure onto a screen.

The screen is coated with a light sensitive emulsion and the film positive is transferred by exposure to ultraviolet light. Black and opaque areas of the image block light, resulting in the emulsion coming away from the mesh during washing out; these are the areas that will print. Light allowed to pass through the emulsion hardens it making it water-resistant. Imagery that is not opaque enough, even in parts, will allow light through, resulting in patchy screen exposure, or the breaking down of the emulsion at an early stage. There are a variety of methods of preparing a film positive:

Hand-drawn images

Specialist polyester film like 'Kodatrace', comes on a roll and is suitable for use with many different media. Photo-opaque, a brown-orange or black 'paint' is ideal for translating drawn designs onto film. It can be applied with brushes and sponges, or comes in pen form for fine lines, to create a variety of textures. It is also possible to scratch into the surface of dried photo-opaque with a scalpel. Film is quite expensive, but as photo-opaque is water-based, it can be washed down and re-used. When storing artwork prepared in this manner, keep flat if possible and in a cool place to prevent photo-opaque from cracking, flaking or becoming sticky. Other materials that are suitable for use on this film include black oil pastel, wax crayon, litho crayon and chinagraph pencil, also black paper or card can be cut out for larger shapes; technical drawing ink can also be used in conjunction with masking fluid as a resist. The film is substantial enough for frottage, by rubbing over textured surfaces with a litho crayon or similar. Linocut designs can be applied directly onto the film with black block-printing ink (or photo-opaque). Because the film is not absorbent, experimentation with the ink consistency is necessary to prevent blotting. Another type of polyester film called 'Truegrain' is very useful as it has a textured surface, improving adhesion of certain waxy materials such as oil pastel and litho crayon. All these methods will produce lines and marks of varying texture and opacity, so exposure time would need to be adjusted accordingly. Always check opacity of the artwork on a light box before exposure.

Masking films

A positive can also be created by cutting a film stencil, using a product like 'Automask' (Sericol). The red or amber film reads as opaque during exposure, but is transparent enough to lay over artwork on a lightbox. You would cut and lay down film onto the Kodatrace as the areas that you wanted to print.

Photocopies

This is a useful method if no other facilities are available although it does not always produce screens of the best quality. Because the photocopied image is of relatively poor density, exposure time has to be longer, to allow light to pass

through the paper and this makes fine or detailed designs difficult to achieve. Imagery can be copied onto ordinary copy paper, which has to be brushed with vegetable oil after copying to make it translucent. This method is only appropriate if no other is available, but the increased exposure time required for light to pass through the paper means that only a bold image is likely to be successful. It is also a messy process, leaving grease on the glass of the exposure unit afterwards. Tracing paper or acetate are much better options for copying onto, and to improve opacity, two or even three layers could be used. However, if the image is large with areas of solid black, it can be difficult to match up the layers for a repeat, as the tracing paper can buckle and distort; acetate is better in this respect. This should be done on a light box to ensure the images match exactly.

Photographic filmwork

Photographically produced artwork will translate onto screen with the greatest accuracy. The traditional method of producing film positives is using a process camera, and in industry these are still used alongside computer systems. Artwork is copied onto high contrast photographic line or lithographic film, which converts the varying tones into either pure black or white. The camera produces a line negative, which is then used to create a full sized positive using one of the techniques below. Film positives can also be made by scanning and manipulating artwork in a computer software programme such as 'Adobe Photoshop' and printed out onto paper, tracing, acetate or film. A printer with 'PostScript' software is necessary for printing half-tones.

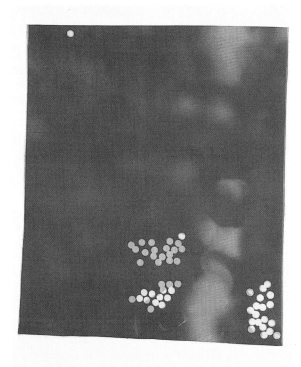

Gillian Stevenson (UK)
Screen-printed with half-tone screen and stencilled
with reactive dyes and discharge on cotton
Photo: Ruth Clark

There are three main methods for making screen-ready photographic positives:

- HALF-TONE: because ink is of a uniform density, it is not possible to produce intermediate tones when printing. By using a 'half-tone screen' during the photographic process, an illusion of varying tones can be created by converting a high contrast image into a series of black dots of varying intensity. A dark area will be represented by dots very close together and for a lighter tone, the dots will be much more spread out. This process is widely used for reproducing photographs in newspapers, magazines and on posters. For screen-printing, the dot size needs to be quite large (measured as number of dots to the square inch), and the mesh size generally not less than 62T (160T). Half tones can be used to re-create any continuous tone image such as drawings and not just photographs. It is a useful method, as you only need one screen; alternatively, by using two screens, one with a positive and one with a negative half-tone image, a very three-dimensional effect print can be produced using, for example, one colour and discharge

- TONE SEPARATION: artwork which contains varying shades of grey is converted into several separate line positives of varying density. Each positive or separation can be used to print a different colour or tone when screen-printed

- FULL COLOUR SEPARATION: colour originals can be used to generate tone separations and half-tone using red, blue and green filters. The filters convert their complimentary colour into a black image on the positive: red turns cyan black / green turns magenta black / blue turns yellow black. If all three colours are used to make three separations, a close approximation of the original can be reproduced if the separations are printed with cyan, yellow and magenta inks. A fourth separation, printing black ink may be needed to give a good black shadow area. Although it is possible to produce a full-colour half-tone image by screen-printing using this method, there is a risk of moiré patterns (interference) between the halftones and screen mesh

This is the process of determining where all the elements in a design recur when the fabric is printed. In order to print a repeat, the design will cover the full width of the fabric (if desired), but is divided into sections lengthways, so that full coverage is achieved through repeated printing down the length of the cloth. There are various repeat systems or networks, which act as (often invisible) structures around which a design is constructed. A successful repeat is where all sides of the repeat unit link up without any visible joins or unwanted tramlines or gaps. There are many types of repeat systems and these are listed below. Four examples are illustrated, the half drop, one of the simplest, being shown in the second method example.

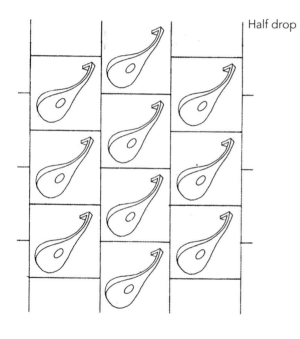

Half drop

FULL DROP – unit can be square or rectangular in format. Each repeat unit is placed exactly next to and below each other.

HALF DROP – unit can be square or rectangular in format. The repeat unit is dropped by half a unit in every other column.

BRICK – unit is rectangular. The repeat unit is moved along by half a unit in every other row.

SPOT – unit is square in format and laid out in a full drop system. The system is derived from sateen weave structures. The repeat unit is divided into a grid of between 3 and 8 squares across and down, with the motif appearing only once in each row or column.

Brick

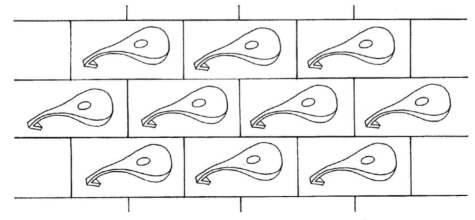

Four spot repeat

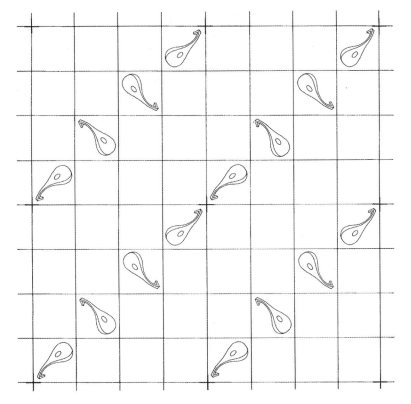

DIAMOND – unit is diamond-shaped.

TRIANGLE – unit is triangular with the overall layout the same as for diamond.

STRIPE – the layout is fundamentally horizontal, vertical or diagonal in format.

HEXAGON – unit is hexagonal in format and arranged in a brick system.

OGEE – unit is a traditional onion shape and laid out in a half drop system.

SCALE – unit is like fish scales and laid out in a half drop system.

MIRROR – an asymmetrical motif is reversed within a square or rectangular repeat unit and laid out in a half drop system.

TURN-OVER – unit is square in format. There are four motifs per repeat unit, each of which is turned over once in each direction from the top left-hand corner. The overall layout is in a full drop system.

SWISS – the design is built up within a diamond shaped repeat unit and developed in a similar way to that of the 'simple' repeat method described. The cut-through line runs both horizontally and vertically, with the four sections repositioned diagonally opposite each other, before the space is filled in. A useful method when putting a drawing into repeat, as well as being suitable for random motifs.

TOSSED – (often several different) motifs are arranged in a random way within the repeat unit and can be loosely or tightly spaced.

ALL-OVER – similar to tossed above, except that the motifs connect in such a way that the pattern unfolds across the fabric.

Designing a repeat can be done manually, or on a computer, either way, the principles are the same. You will need to use a grid to lay out the motifs accurately unless you are using a software package specifically designed for textile design,

125

A simple repeat; the design is developed over the full width of cloth.

cut-through line

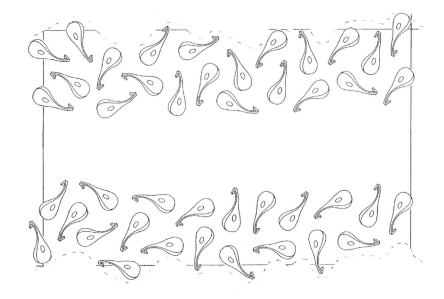

width of cloth (selvedge to selvedge)

After cutting, the design is reversed, leaving a space to fill in with remaining motifs.

The distance between the two cut edges is the repeat size and each end should be marked with a registration cross.

repeat size

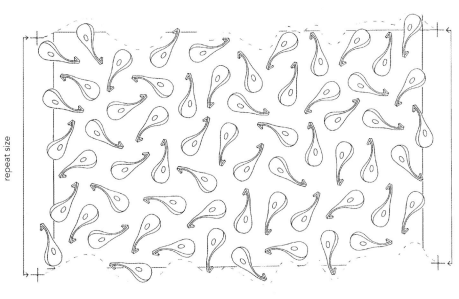

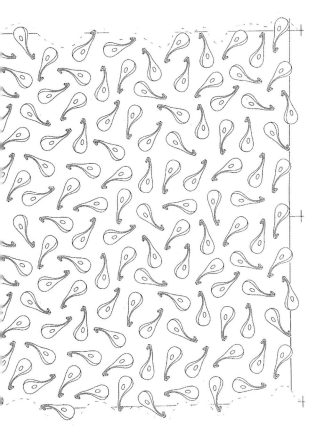

The repeat unit is traced and positioned correctly below, matching registration crosses, to check that all elements of the repeat are balanced

which allows you to place motifs in all the different repeat networks quickly and easily. 'Lectra U4ia' is one such commercial package used by large textile companies.

There are several methods of putting a design into repeat and two approaches are described here. The first outlines a simple technique where the design is developed over the full width of the cloth. Although not used in industry, this procedure is a useful way of understanding how a repeat works. The second is for a full drop repeat using a 'repeat unit', and these principles can be applied for any of the other repeat systems.

When working out your repeat manually you will need large sheets of graph and tracing paper (buying them on a roll is easiest), as well as masking tape, spray mount and a sharp pencil or fine biro. If a light-box is available, then this makes the task much easier. Beware of using photocopies of your original design when working out repeats, as they will not be 100% accurate.

A SIMPLE REPEAT

This is particularly suitable for a random effect, using individual motifs at any scale. However, one has to be very careful to create a balanced design without unwanted gaps or lines appearing.

1   First you need to measure and cut out your graph and tracing paper. They should be slightly wider and longer than the width and depth of your repeat. For example, to print on fabric 120cm wide, you might use a screen with a maximum image size of 150cm x 90cm, with your repeat depth being around 70cm. Therefore, cut the papers to measure about 130cm x 80cm.

2   Tape down the graph paper onto a table or light box, and secure a sheet of tracing paper over the top.

3   Measure the required width, in this case 120cm, and draw two vertical lines down each side of the tracing paper, using the graph paper behind as a guide. These lines represent the selvedge edges of your fabric.

4   Measure the central point of these lines and draw a horizontal line across the width of the tracing paper.

5   You are now ready to start arranging your individual motifs around this central line. Gradually build up the design across the full width (120cm) of the cloth, but keep the depth at about 50cm, that is, about 25cm each side of

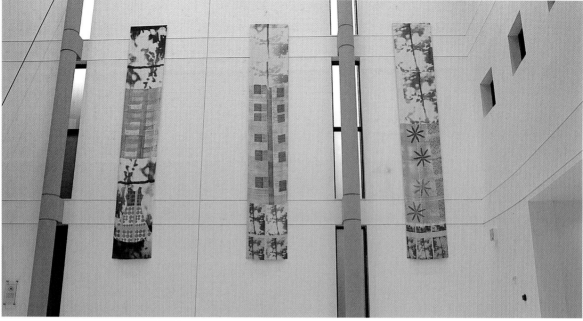

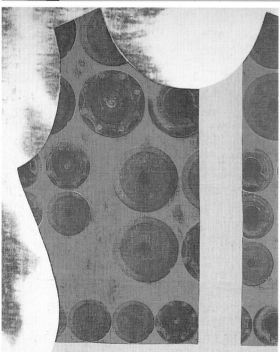

Joanna Kinnersly-Taylor (UK)
TOP AND DETAIL ABOVE Three of a series of four wall-hangings sited in the atrium of the new block at the Mater Hospital, Belfast; commissioned by the Mater Hospital Trust with funding from the National Lottery through the Arts Council of Northern Ireland; 2001 Dyed and screen-printed with reactive dyes and discharge on Irish linen – Each 100cm x 600cm
Photo: Ruth Clark

the central line. Stick down the images using a light coating of spray mount, as this makes them easy to move and reposition as necessary.

6 Next you will need to locate the best place for the 'cut-through' line, which will ultimately put the design into repeat. The line should be drawn from one (selvedge) edge to the other, utilising natural breaks and avoiding going through the centre of images. If you are going to be doing colour separations, then each of these will require its own cut-though line, although they will all follow a similar route.

7 Once the cut-through line has been established, cut and reverse the design, so that the lower half is repositioned above the top half, with the two cut edges becoming the outer edges. Leave a space of about 20cm into which additional motifs will be placed to complete the design (the exact depth of the gap will depend on the scale of the motifs). Take care to ensure the design remains square, by matching up the vertical lines on the tracing paper, and join the two halves together with magic tape.

8 Once the remaining motifs have been arranged within the space, you can work out the repeat size. Measure the distance between the two cut edges and mark with registration crosses at each end on both selvedge edges. The completed design in this form is called the 'layout'.

9 In order to check the design is balanced and fits together properly (sometimes called proving), trace the whole design (include vertical lines and registration crosses, but you can omit details in the motifs) onto another piece of tracing paper and position below the first, matching everything up correctly. If there are any discrepancies, then now is the time to make alterations.

10 The layout is now ready to be translated into suitable positive(s) for transferral to screen using one of the methods described previously; (also see text opposite, 'Full drop using...').

CREATING A REPEAT USING A REPEAT UNIT

With this method, the motif(s) are arranged within a 'repeat unit', which is duplicated across the width of the cloth in the desired repeat system format or grid. Because you are creating the design within a repeat unit, everything automatically repeats and there is normally no need for a cut-through line. The exception to this would be with larger, solid areas of design at the top or bottom edges of the repeat unit, such as geometric shapes, that substantially connect to each other when repeated. Here a cut-through line may be desirable, as a wavy line helps to disguise the join better than a straight one. If this approach is adopted, obviously the design is cut and reversed exactly, without leaving a gap to fill in.

FULL DROP USING A REPEAT UNIT

A full drop repeat is where each repeat unit is placed exactly next to and below each other.

1 From the width of your cloth you will be printing on, work out a suitable size grid to work from. For example, if you are going to print on cloth 120cm wide, you could have four x 30cm wide units (4 x 30 = 120), six x 20cm units, eight x 15cm units and so on, depending on the scale of your motifs. The repeat units can be square or rectangular in format and can be any size. In this example, the repeat unit measures 20cm wide x 58cm high.

2 Tape down the graph paper onto a table or light box, and secure a sheet of tracing paper over the top. To accommodate the design example, these should measure about 130cm wide x 126cm deep.

3 Using the graph paper underneath as a guide, carefully draw out your required full drop

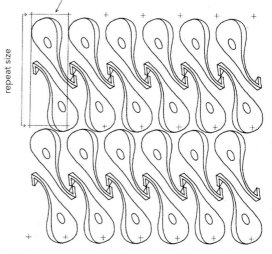

repeat unit – draw the first one as a complete rectangle or square and mark the remainder with a cross at each corner

repeat size

A full drop repeat; the design is developed within a repeat unit and there is normally no need for a cut-through line as everything automatically repeats. This method can be adapted to suit all types of repeat systems.

grid. The first unit should be drawn completely with the remainder denoted by marking a cross at each corner. In this example, the grid comprises two rows of rectangles each 20cm x 58cm, one above the other.

4   Draw your design into the first unit. The exact approach of this stage will depend upon your motifs and the kind of feel you want your print to have. In this example, the two lutes extend beyond the boundaries of the rectangle so that when the unit is duplicated, the motifs interlock and have a strong directional feel.

- If your design is more complex, eg. a plant form with wavy lines that physically joins the adjacent repeat units, this can be achieved through both taking the motif to the edge of the unit or beyond it

- The important thing to remember is that once any image extends beyond the unit boundaries, you must ensure that the shapes either interlock correctly or overlap directly, as desired, otherwise the pattern will not fit together

- If you have lots of smaller motifs arranged in a more random composition, these would overlap the grid lines only slightly, to help prevent unwanted gaps appearing in the overall design layout. The easiest way of arranging random motifs in a repeat unit is to initially build them up along the top and left hand side of the first unit. You would then trace them (in this example), into the second, seventh and eighth units, filling in the gap in the first unit in much the same way as the 'simple' repeat method described earlier

5   Trace the first image onto three smaller pieces of tracing paper, (remember to include the four crosses that denote the corners of the unit so that the image can be accurately posi-

tioned), and tape these in the second, seventh and eighth units. This will give you a sense of how the design fits together and you can make any alterations or additions to the design in the first unit if necessary.

6   Once you are happy with the design, transfer it into all the units by tracing through directly onto the large sheet of tracing paper.

7   Using this method, the depth of the repeat is simply the height of the repeat unit, in this case 58cm. Although the layout shows two rows of repeat units, due to the depth of the repeat, only the first row would be put onto a screen.

The next stage is to prepare a screen positive using one of the methods described previously. Remember that for a multi-coloured design, a separate positive is needed for each colour to be printed. If you are working in Adobe Photoshop, positives can be printed out complete with registration crosses, providing the page size is large enough to accommodate them. However, always check registration on a light box and with all positives, an identifying word or symbol should be marked on the bottom right-hand side of each positive (as below).

For hand-drawn imagery:

1   Tape down a sheet of Kodatrace on the light box over the design layout. Transfer the registration crosses top and bottom onto the Kodatrace.

2   As a general rule, the first positive is the one which has the least coverage. However, if this colour is a highlight, which will be printed over everything else, it would be painted last.

3   For each subsequent colour, superimpose a new sheet of Kodatrace over the last, marking the four registration crosses each time, so all the colour separations match up exactly. In the

bottom right-hand corner write an identifying word or symbol, that can only be read in one and the same way on each positive; this is to help correct positioning of positives on the screen at registration and exposure stage. If there are areas in the design where colours butt up against each other, allow a very small overlap of about 1mm. A greater overlap may create an unsightly darker line of a different colour.

4 Check the opacity of the positives and only remove from the light-box when everything is finished.

In selecting a screen, see the notes on page 133 for hints on sizes. The following methods assume the screen mesh has been stretched professionally, i.e. that it is very taut and can withstand the use of a high pressure hose. Because hazardous chemicals are involved, it is very important to ensure good ventilation and to wear gloves, mask and goggles for these processes.

DEGREASING

New screen mesh should be degreased to remove grease and impurities and also to roughen the mesh, enabling the emulsion to properly adhere to it. Existing screens also benefit from periodic degreasing, to keep them in the best condition. This degreasing detergent comes in either a liquid form – ideal for general screen maintenance, or as a paste, which is best for brand-new mesh. A suitable degreaser can be obtained from your screen-printing supplier.

The mesh should be thoroughly wetted and degreaser applied to both sides of the screen. It is left for a few minutes and then rinsed off with a high-pressure hose.

If you get a 'moiré' effect when printing with a

Applying stencil remover and using a power hose to blast away old emulsion

131

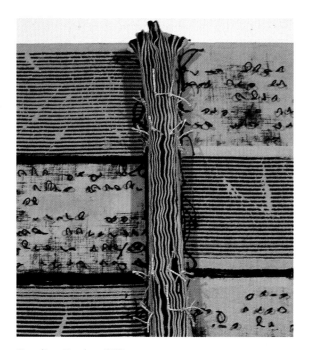

Caroline Bartlett (UK)
'Untitled' (detail from triptych), 2000
Black linen with flour paste and stitch resist, discharge
printed and painted, pleated centre panels
198cm x 26cm Crafts Council Collection
Photo: Andy Monks

new screen, this is a sign that your screen has not
been properly degreased.

RECLAIMING A SCREEN

In order to remove imagery from a screen so that
it can be reused, you will need to obtain a stripper that is suitable for removing the particular
type of emulsion it is coated with. Each brand of
emulsion will have a compatible stripper, and
you should follow manufacturer's instructions.
The following procedure is designed for optimum stripping of a screen coated with Ulano
emulsion (on the outside of the screen only) and
serves as a guide to the general process.

1 All tape must be removed from the screen.
  Wet gummed tape thoroughly with a hose

and leave for 3–5 minutes. Repeat the process,
after which the tape should peel away fairly
easily. Stubborn bits of tape can be blasted
away with a high pressure hose (but take care
not to block the drain).

2 Dilute the stripper, following manufacturer's
instructions; only mix as much as you need.
For Ulano, a dilution of about 1 part stripper
to 20–25 parts water works well.

3 Wet the screen on both sides. Use (ideally) a
thin cellulose sponge to apply the stripper fairly
generously to first the outside and then the inside of the screen. Rub the sponge vigorously
over the mesh, ensuring even coverage. Leave
for 2–3 minutes, depending on ambient temperature. Do not exceed this or allow the stripper to dry on the mesh, as the emulsion will
harden and become impossible to remove.

4 Using a high pressure hose, blast away the soft-
ened emulsion from the *inside* of the screen
first. Work methodically, from one side of the
screen to the other and from the bottom of the
screen upwards. If done the other way around,
particularly on a large screen, water running
down dilutes the stripper, causing it to be less
effective. Hold the hose fairly close to the
mesh, particularly with stubborn areas of
emulsion. After a while, turn the screen
around and blast onto the outside of the mesh.

NOTE:
• It is extremely important that when using the
power hose you first turn on the water and
then the power, reversing the order when
switching off. NEVER leave one on without
the other, and always switch both off when
not in use. Do not leave water and power on
without using hose for more than a few seconds (eg. when turning a screen round).

5 The emulsion should wash out fairly easily within a few minutes and the screen should be held up to the light to check for any blockages. It is important to be thorough, as if the mesh is not completely clean, it can cause problems later on.

6 If the emulsion has been on the screen for a long time, it may be difficult to remove, in which case, the process can be repeated.

7 If there are still areas that will not wash out, the next step is to use a caustic paste, which is stronger than the liquid stripper. This is applied and left on the screen for a few minutes before washing out with the pressure hose.

8 Staining of the mesh will not affect the imagery on the screen, but removal may be preferred (especially if doing half-tone work). A 'haze remover' can be applied and this is left for several hours or overnight. Staining is a problem particularly caused by using pigment inks.

REGISTERING SCREENS FOR A REPEAT DESIGN

This has to be done prior to coating and exposure.

1 Also see Chapter 11, 'Attaching the bracket to the screen'.
  Initially lay the clean, dry screen on the print table so that it is flat against the registration rail.

NOTES:
- If you are going to be using bulkier adjustable 'clamps' instead of brackets when you come to print, you may wish to put these on temporarily at this stage for absolute accuracy when measuring. This is because you will need to take into account the increased distance that the screen will sit from the rail. Remember to

remove the clamps once the screen is registered (prior to exposure), but *do not adjust the clamp mechanism which sets the distance from the rail*

- If you are using an ordinary bracket on the screen, the distance the screen sits from the rail is much smaller, determined only by the amount the stop protrudes from the rail (approximately 1–1.5cm). Again, for accuracy, you may wish to position a couple of stops against which to place the screen at this measuring stage

- From this, determine how far in from the rail the positives need to be positioned, in order to provide a 'well' for the print paste of (ideally) at least 12–15cm at each end of the screen. If using a number of screens with different frame depths, base this measurement on the deepest framed screen. In selecting a screen, remember to also allow a minimum of about 6cm at each side, to allow the squeegee to be pulled evenly and smoothly across the screen. Make a note of the distance from the rail to the start of the design for subsequent reference when ironing down/pinning out cloth

- If printing a design that is significantly narrower than the width of cloth and you wish to centre the design, take this into account when positioning artwork onto the screen by allowing enough space for cloth (that will be unprinted) to be positioned on the rail side

2 Move the screen and stick down a length of newsprint across the width of and down the table (enough to cover the depth of repeat) onto which measurements can be marked.

3 Use a set square to measure the required distance from the registration rail, drawing a line in fine biro parallel to the rail on the newsprint. Using a large steel ruler against a

Measuring and marking a right angle on to newsprint

line drawn on newsprint in fine biro at the required distance from, and parallel to the regestration rail; draw a horizontal line across the table at right angles to the first line.

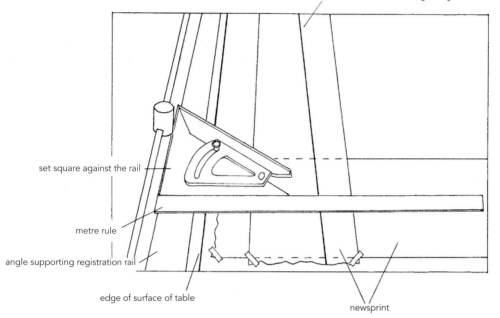

set square against the rail

metre rule

angle supporting registration rail

edge of surface of table

newsprint

Transferring registration crosses on the positive to the screen

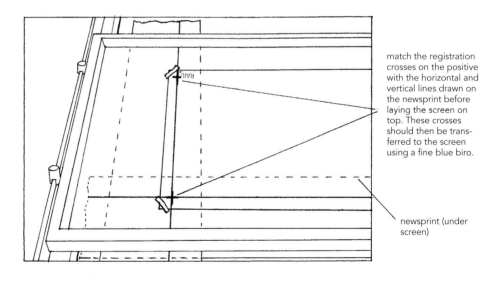

match the registration crosses on the positive with the horizontal and vertical lines drawn on the newsprint before laying the screen on top. These crosses should then be transferred to the screen using a fine blue biro.

newsprint (under screen)

set square held against the rail, draw another line at a right angle to the last, the full width of the repeat, again on the newsprint.

4 Use masking tape to position the first positive on the table, so that the registration crosses are square to the right angle, and the identifying word or symbol is at the rail side.

NOTE:

• A tracing paper positive can be awkward to position accurately, as it does not lie completely flat. If the screen is large, get someone to help position it, so that the artwork does not buckle

5 Next place the screen over the positive, ensuring

the frame is right up against the rail or stops, or that clamps are in position. Centre the design on the screen if possible, although if there are imperfections in the screen mesh, the image can be positioned to avoid them. If the repeat depth is very shallow in comparison to the screen size, you may wish to position imagery nearer to one edge of the screen (depending on whether you print from left to right or right to left down the table), so that as you print, the screen will not touch the previous wet print

6 Carefully transfer the four registration crosses, as well as the identifying word or symbol on the positive, to the screen using a blue biro and a ruler for accuracy. This mark ensures correct and consistent positioning of positives on all screens before exposure.

7 For colour separations, register all subsequent screens to the *same* positive, already on the table, (you have already registered them to each other on the light box). It does not matter if the frames vary in size, or if each colour positive is further up or down the screen, as long as the transferred crosses drawn on the mesh are all in the *same position in relation to the rail.* All the screens should now be marked with four crosses and the identifying word or symbol written by the lower right-hand cross, ready for exposure.

COATING A SCREEN

If you are coating screens for a repeat image, it is essential to first register the screen(s).

There are many different types of photographic emulsion on the market and it is therefore important to choose one that will suit your particular needs. Emulsion comes in two parts: the emulsion itself and the sensitiser, which, when added to the emulsion, makes it light sensitive. This means the emulsion must always be handled in darkroom conditions. The sensitiser normally comes in a small bottle, to which water is added and then shaken to dissolve. This solution is then thoroughly stirred into the emulsion, which should be left to stand for a few hours to eliminate all air bubbles. Once the emulsion has been sensitised, it has a shelf life, the length of which depends on the particular brand and storage conditions. For example, 'Ulano', an American brand of emulsion, will last for up to about 4 months once sensitised, providing it is kept in a cool, dark place. However, it is worth remembering that the fresher the sensitised emulsion is, the more readily it washes out after exposure. It may therefore be helpful to use up older emulsion on bolder designs with solid areas of colour, and the fresher one with fine or half-tone images. It is also useful to have a small jar of old emulsion for touching up screens after exposure. Always write the date of sensitising on the emulsion. If you use emulsion fairly infrequently, and you have a spare container, it may be worth halving the emulsion and only sensitising one half at a time. Dissolve all the sensitiser and measure out half; the remainder should keep satisfactorily in a dissolved state.

The exact coating method adopted will depend on the type of emulsion used – some brands require/recommend coating on the inside *and* outside of the screen; follow the manufacturer's instructions and do a small test screen when using emulsion for the first time. For simplicity, the following coating method uses 'Ulano' emulsion and has been adapted from the manufacturer's instructions to suit the particular situation I work in, although the basic principle will be similar for other brands. *Always* wear rubber gloves when handling photographic emulsion as it contains hazardous chemicals.

The following procedure should be carried out in subdued lighting, or preferably a darkroom.

1 Ensure that your screen is clean and dry (see section on reclaiming a screen).
2 Select a coating trough that is suitable for the size of your screen. Ideally, the length of the trough should be about 2–3cm narrower than the width of the mesh to give a smooth, even coating. Do not use a trough larger than about 80cm long, as it will be difficult to control, resulting in uneven coating. If coating a screen that exceeds this size, use a smaller trough and apply in two halves, ensuring that there is an overlap of emulsion. Apply the emulsion as close as possible to all the edges. This means the gum strip will not get excessively wet each time the screen is washed out after printing, reducing the possibility of print paste seepage.
3 Pour the sensitised emulsion carefully and slowly into the coating trough (to avoid making air bubbles); make sure there is enough emulsion to cover the screen in one movement, but do not overfill. Wipe any drips off the outside of the trough with a damp cloth.
4 Lean the screen against a wall at an angle of about 25°–30°, with the *outside* of the screen facing you. (If you are coating a large screen, it may be necessary to get someone to hold it for you; a small screen may need to be held with one hand and coated with the other). Starting at the bottom of the screen, hold the trough firmly (ideally) with both hands, at the edge of the mesh and tilt slightly to ensure

Coating a large screen with emulsion; a medium-sized trough is used to apply the emulsion in two halves

emulsion is in contact with the screen mesh. Then firmly and smoothly, push the trough up the height of the screen, ensuring there is a steady flow of emulsion but do not tilt the trough too severely. Stop at the inside edge of the frame at the top and tilt the trough slightly away from the screen again, so that the emulsion runs back into the trough.
5 Repeat step 4, this time holding the trough level, so no further coating is transferred onto the screen. This helps remove any excess or uneven coating, but take care not to remove too much emulsion, as the coating will be too thin and not receive the image properly or break down when washing out.

6 Use a plastic spatula to scrape excess coating from the trough back into the container. Wash the trough and any utensils immediately after use, as any emulsion remaining will set hard. If there is any emulsion on the screen frame, wipe this off carefully with a damp cloth.

7 The coated screen should now be left to dry horizontally in a warm room or drying cupboard (remember it still needs to be in dark room conditions). Do not expose the screen to excessive amounts of heat as the emulsion can start to harden and will not wash out properly after exposure. If drying in a rack, position freshly coated screens *below* dry ones, in case of drips. Depending on the size of screen and room temperature, drying time ranges from approximately 45 minutes to 2 hours.

Optimum results are achieved by exposing the screen within 24 hours of coating. However, if the screen is dried naturally and kept in a cool darkroom, it may be possible to leave it for up to about a week, depending on brand of emulsion.

EXPOSING A SCREEN

Exposure time will depend very much on the type of exposure unit and the strength of its light source, the brand of emulsion and the quality of the positive. Generally speaking, the more opaque and solid the image, the shorter the exposure, with detailed designs in less opaque media requiring a longer period. It is important not to expose screens for too short a period as the emulsion will be unstable and form pinholes or peel away in sections during washing out. Likewise, too long an exposure will result in the emulsion becoming very difficult or impossible to wash out.

As a rule, the more basic the exposure unit and weaker the light source, the longer the exposure time. For example, a home-made unit using fluorescent tubes may take up to 15 or 20 minutes, whereas most colleges use units with a power source of around 2-3kW, resulting in exposure times of between 30 seconds up to about $2\frac{1}{2}$ minutes. With the more sophisticated units with a light source of say, between 5-6kW, (used in industry and some colleges), exposure time is measured in 'light units' rather than seconds or minutes. This is because as the bulbs degrade, length of exposure time is automatically increased to compensate for the slight loss of power. Here a minimum exposure time may be measured as '30 light units'. These exposure units tend to be bigger, as the increased power is used to spread light over a greater area to accommodate exposure of very large screens.

It is helpful to keep a record noting exposure times for positives in different media and on what size screen mesh. When using equipment for the first time, do a small test screen gradually exposing the artwork to longer periods of exposure. Photo-opaque on Kodatrace is the ideal medium for the test screen positive, as the correct exposure time for this will be a marker to judge exposure times for other types of artwork. Paint up a simple design measuring about 36cm x 10cm, incorporating a variety of marks and divide into six sections. Cut out some black paper exactly the same size and cover all but one section of the design. Tape the Kodatrace and black paper onto the screen and expose for a set number of seconds or minutes (depending on the strength of the light source). Then move the black paper along so that the second section is revealed and expose again for the same amount

APPROXIMATE GUIDE TO EXPOSURE TIMES

The following are all subject to type of unit, strength of power source, brand of emulsion and quality of positive

Type of artwork	Approximate length of exposure with a 3kW light source sited 1.25–1.5m from vacuum frame
photo-opaque on Kodatrace	2–2 ½ minutes
photo-opaque on Kodatrace – fine lines and detail	1 minute 45 seconds – 2 minutes 15 seconds
filmwork	2 minutes – 2 minutes 15 seconds
filmwork – fine lines and detail	1 minute 40 seconds – 2 minutes
black oil pastel, wax crayon, lithocrayon, chinagraph lithocrayon, chinagraph	1 minute 40 seconds – 2 minutes
photocopy on acetate (may increase time if using 2 or 3 layers together)	1 minute 40 seconds – 2 minutes
photocopy on tracing paper	1 minute 40 seconds – 1 minute 50 seconds
photocopy on oiled photocopy paper (only suitable with a bold image and if no other method is available)	2 ½–3 minutes

of time. Continue until all six sections have been exposed, the first section having received the longest exposure (six times that of the first), and the last, the shortest time.

When exposing several different images onto one screen, make sure that there are no overlapping areas of Kodatrace and allow some space around each image, so that areas can be masked off easily. Only combine images that are compatible in terms of exposure time. Position images 'square' to the screen as it is easier to position imagery at the right angle when placement printing.

Use 'magic tape' instead of sellotape when attaching artwork to the screen for exposure; it is easier to remove and doesn't become sticky with the heat of the lights.

The following should also be carried out in subdued lighting or darkroom conditions.

1 Check that the screen coating is completely dry and stick the positive face down onto the *outside* of the screen, matching exactly all crosses and identification mark, if doing a repeat.

2 Check that the glass of the exposure unit is clean and grease-free and place the screen, *artwork side down* onto the middle of the glass. Lower and secure the lid, turn on the vacuum pump and wait for the black rubber blanket to completely suck down around the screen. If using a light box without a vacuum pump, place a piece of foam inside the screen (it should fit as closely as possible) and lay a piece of wood the same size on top of this. Then place heavy weights on top of the wood; this will ensure good contact between the positive and the screen.

3 If the unit has an automatic timer, set this to the required exposure time. Turn off any lighting and draw the blackout curtain. Turn on the light source and expose the screen for the required time.

A vacuum frame is used in conjunction with a UV light source used in a separate unit to expose screens at Double Elephant's studio

IMPORTANT:

If using ultraviolet as the light source, it is very important not to expose your eyes to this damaging light.

After exposure, turn off the vacuum and wait á few moments for the rubber blanket to release, then lift the lid, remove the screen and take off the positive.

WASHING OUT A SCREEN

The washing out process should be done immediately after exposure and can be done in normal lighting conditions.

1 Use a hose and start with fairly low water pressure and cold water. Wet the screen gently on both sides for a few moments, working over the whole surface.

2 Turn the screen so that the *inside* is facing you and move the hose back and forth across the mesh evenly. You should see a faint impression of the image appearing quite quickly, but it may take time for the actual emulsion to wash away from the areas to be printed. This will depend on the quality of the image and the length of exposure time; the shorter the exposure, the more fragile the emulsion and the image.

3 Continue until the whole image has washed out. Check that there is no excess emulsion, as this can cause a blockage if left to dry on the mesh. Gently run your fingers over the inside surface of the screen; if it feels slimy, it needs more washing. Hold the screen up to the light to check that there are no blockages and that all parts of the image have properly washed out. Allow to dry thoroughly.

NOTES:

If it becomes apparent after some time that the image is not appearing, several things can be done:

- increase the water pressure
- increase the water temperature
- use a cloth to gently rub at the areas on the inside of the screen which are not washing out
- hose the *outside* of the screen
- as a last resort, use a high-pressure hose on the inside of the screen. This may cause the image and emulsion to break down

If none of the above work, the only thing to do is reclaim the screen and start again. The quality of the positive probably needs to be improved, or the exposure time could be reduced.

APPLYING GUMMED TAPE

Once the screen is dry, the next stage is to apply gummed tape (a brown paper tape with gum on the shiny side) around all four edges of the outside of the screen. Brown, shiny parcel tape may also be used, if preferred, although this can be difficult to remove at the reclamation stage, especially if it has been on the screen for a long time. The tape blocks off the small areas of open mesh between the frame and emulsion. Gummed or parcel tape measuring 46–50mm (2in.) wide is an ideal size. Cut a total of 8 lengths of tape for each screen, (2 strips for each side), making each piece about 2cm shorter than the width or height of the screen. Wet the tape with a sponge or run through a jug of water, squeezing off excess moisture by running two fingers down the tape (this helps

▲ Applying gummed tape to the screen
◀ Fiona Claydon (UK)
Reactive dyed, screen-printed colour discharge, discharge and pigment on silk
(BELOW) Sara Robertson (UK)
Hand-painted and screen-printed furnishing cotton with pigment dyes
Photo: Evan Hughes

prevent gum dripping onto open mesh and causing blockages). Starting at the outside edges, work around the screen in one direction, laying on one piece of tape at a time, so that each piece overlaps the last at each corner. Partly overlap the second layers of tape over the first to create a strong mask. If the emulsion was applied as close to the edges as possible, then the gum strip will be able to withstand repeated washing without water penetrating it. Hold the screen up to the light again, to check there are no blockages caused by dripping gum; if so, wipe with a clean, damp cloth.

NOTE:

- If printing through a blank screen, using stencils or resist techniques, it is better to use parcel tape, as gum strip will not withstand washing out very well (as there is no emulsion to protect it). Remember to create enough space for an ink well at each end

TOUCHING UP THE SCREEN

Next the screen should be checked for pinholes or imperfections in the emulsion. Lay the screen face up on a light-box or stand on a windowsill. Use a small brush to apply emulsion, which may be watered-down a little if necessary. Paint out any unwanted gaps in the emulsion and allow to dry. A small piece of stiff card may also be used to spread the emulsion in a thin, even layer.

Ensure the touched-up areas and the gummed tape are completely dry before printing.

NOTE:

- If desired, the screen can be 're-exposed' for a few minutes to further harden the emulsion. This can be advantageous with fragile images that had a short exposure time

CHAPTER ELEVEN

PRINTING

PREPARATION

SETTING THE REGISTRATION STOPS FOR A REPEAT PRINT

Before laying down the cloth on the table, it is necessary to set the stops on the registration rail.

1 Check the repeat size; this will be marked on your design layout (Chapter 10).
2 Use a metal ruler and stick a small piece of masking tape on the ruler at the correct repeat size. This ensures repeated accurate measuring.
3 The stops are set by measuring the repeat size from the left-hand side of one stop, to the left-hand side of the next stop, or from the right-hand side to right-hand side. I find it easier to measure from the left-hand side, as the ruler is supported by the stops and you can feel with your finger if the left-hand end of the ruler matches the edge of the stop. Either way, be consistent, as at this stage it is easy to make a mistake. Work down the table, measuring and fixing the stops into place. Put the allen key into the stop *before* measuring, and turn carefully so that there is minimal movement as you tighten them up. Once all stops are in place, check again that distances are correct.

ATTACHING THE BRACKET TO THE SCREEN

A bracket or clamp is absolutely essential if the design fits together very precisely, otherwise it may be possible to just use pieces of masking tape as markers on the screen frame to match against stops. There are various types of brackets and clamps for screens, depending on the type of frame. At its simplest, a bracket can be a piece of steel flat bar that screws into the rail end of the screen frame and extends enough beyond the frame to sit firmly against each stop. A bracket is normally positioned on the right-hand side of the screen, sitting against the left-hand side of the stop, although it does not matter if the reverse is done, as long as the process is consistent.

Adjustable clamps may also be used and are particularly useful on metal frames with no means of fixing and can be utilised on a variety of frame depths. The example shown here is made from up-turned mild steel channel with a bar welded on top. A small section of tube with a flat, inverse 'L' shaped plate welded at the rail end slides along this with a threaded bolt to tighten and fix it in position at the required distance from, and with the plate butting up against, the rail.

Diagram of a clamp; two can be used instead of a bracket

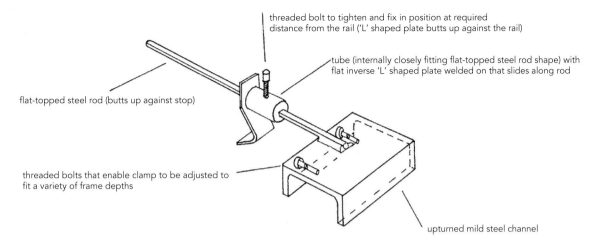

threaded bolt to tighten and fix in position at required distance from the rail ('L' shaped plate butts up against the rail)

tube (internally closely fitting flat-topped steel rod shape) with flat inverse 'L' shaped plate welded on that slides along rod

flat-topped steel rod (butts up against stop)

threaded bolts that enable clamp to be adjusted to fit a variety of frame depths

upturned mild steel channel

If you are going to be using a simple metal bracket which is screwed directly into the screen frame, the screen will sit flush against the stops. The bracket is not put on until the stops are set, once the screen has been exposed

Position of screen in relation to registration rail using adjustable clamps

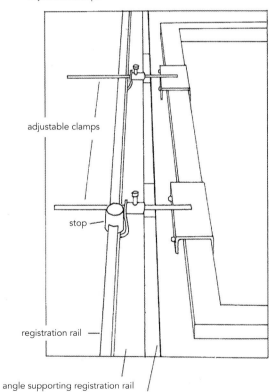

adjustable clamps

stop

registration rail

angle supporting registration rail

edge of surface of table

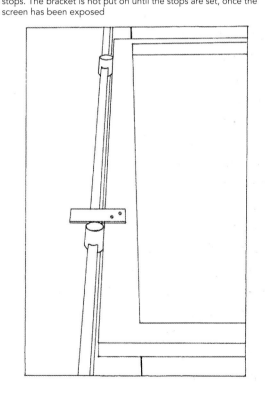

This clamp design was devised by Ivor Laycock at Glasgow School of Art and is based on those used in larger print works.

Clamps are also helpful if you wish to position a smaller screen some distance from the rail, for example, to centre a design on wide cloth.

Because the design of an adjustable clamp means the screen sits further away from the rail (approximately 10cm +) than if using a bracket, it is necessary to use two clamps on each screen to ensure the screen remains parallel to the rail each time it is moved and repositioned.

First, position the screen centrally between two stops and attach the bracket or first clamp so that it butts up against the left hand side of the right hand stop. If using clamps, position the second one at approximately an equal distance in from the other end of the screen ensuring it does not clash with the next stop. The bracket or clamps should now remain in place for the whole of the printing process, ie. each screen should have its own bracket or pair of clamps.

For designs with several colours, start by fixing a bracket on the screen with the most imagery on it. Print this screen onto newsprint taped firmly to the table, allow to dry, and then lay down the next screen against the stops, so that it lines up correctly with the first print. Then fix the bracket onto the screen as before. Print this next screen and repeat the process, lining up the remaining screens in the same way.

POSITIONING CLOTH FOR A REPEAT PRINT

For a repeating design, the cloth needs to be positioned at the correct distance from and parallel to the registration rail. Lay the screen on the table against the pre-set stops, and check the distance from the rail to where the design starts (you will have made a note of this earlier). Then use a set-square against the rail to measure the correct distance and draw a line down the table (parallel to the rail), on which the cloth will be positioned using one of the methods below. Remember that if the cloth is wider than the design and you wish to centre the image, take this into account when measuring the distance from the rail.

PREPARING THE PRINT TABLE

The print table should be totally clean and dry before use. There are three main methods of fixing the cloth to the surface of the table. The chosen method will depend on thickness and type of fabric being printed on, and whether the cloth will be lifted on and off the table repeatedly, or removed after one printing session, as with a repeat printed length.

Taping

Using brown parcel tape, cloth can be tensioned and stuck directly to the neoprene surface of the table as shown below.

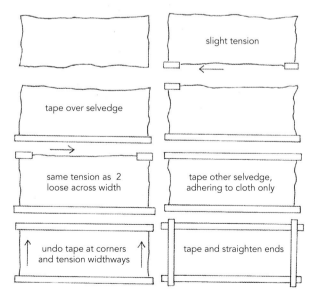

slight tension

tape over selvedge

same tension as 2 loose across width

tape other selvedge, adhering to cloth only

undo tape at corners and tension widthways

tape and straighten ends

Taping cloth directly to the table

Gumming the table

The other two methods require the table to be gummed. Select a large squeegee about 70–80cm long and pour a small quantity of gum in a line, the length of the squeegee, onto one end of the table. Use the squeegee to take the gum up one side of the table and down the other, before going down the middle. Keep moving the gum around until it has been distributed in an *even* layer with no thick blobs; make sure the table is well-coated, but also that the gum is not too thick. Wipe away any pools of gum that may have accumulated at the edges of the table, and allow to dry thoroughly, using a fan heater if necessary.

Ironing down the backing cloth

Ironing cloth directly to the table

Cloth may then be ironed down directly onto the gummed surface; this is a very good way of ensuring the cloth remains totally stable during printing, and can be especially useful for hand-painting onto certain fabrics. Make sure that the iron is clean and set to the correct temperature for the fabric, taking care not to distort the cloth during ironing. Start from one end of the cloth, always working from the middle outwards, gradually working up the full length. Some fine, delicate or devoré fabrics may be unsuitable for this method. When the print is dry, peel away the cloth very carefully.

Ironing down a backing cloth

A backing cloth is normally made from cotton duck (see Chapter 2) and is ironed down onto the gummed table surface using a hot iron, enabling fabric to be pinned into it (but not the table). It is a very useful method if cloth is to be taken on and off the table, as for sampling or printing a one-off piece, which has various printing stages. If printing a fine or delicate fabric, the print quality can be improved by having an absorbent backing cloth underneath. The backing cloth should be washed regularly so no paste residue is transferred to work. Pinning cloth may be unsuitable for certain fabrics or print effects. Always use long, fine dressmaking pins with a small head, as these should not damage the screen during printing.

NOTE:
• When ironing cloth onto a gummed table, take care at the edges, where the iron may come into contact with the neoprene surface.

CHECKLIST BEFORE PRINTING

Have you done the following:

- checked for pinholes in the screen
- selected a squeegee that is the correct size
- test-printed the screen to make sure that is clear of emulsion or gummed tape residue
- checked print paste is the correct consistency for the design/fabric
- checked how many pulls are needed
- tested the print pastes fully, i.e. printed, steamed and washed off, to check the colours are correct and fresh

- got masking tape to hand to cover up any missed pinholes
- got a clean, damp cloth to hand

and if printing a repeat:

- put brackets on all screens
- registered screens correctly; and if doing a multi-colour repeat, that the screens have all been lined up to each other
- checked the stops are set at the correct repeat size

PRINTING

There are many factors that will affect the quality of the print, which is why it is so important to sample first. Depending on your stature, it is normally possible to print on your own with a screen up to about 125cm x 65cm. You may need to climb up onto the table and rest your knees on the edge of the frame to secure the screen; heavy weights could also be put at each corner – bricks are ideal. If printing a larger screen or a repeat, then you will need someone else to whom the squeegee will be passed half way across the screen. This should be done is a smooth action, with each person holding the squeegee at the same angle (roughly 75° to the screen), and applying a similar amount of pressure. Printing at too steep an angle results in the flexibility of the squeegee being impaired with insufficient paste deposit; too low an angle means too much paste may be deposited. Likewise a sharp edged squeegee should be used at a steeper angle and a round edged blade at a lower angle. The number of pulls and pressure will depend on thickness of cloth, print paste consistency, type of image and effect desired. If the squeegee is only slightly wider than the design to be printed, keep your eye on *one side* of the squeegee only during printing and this helps ensure you pull the ink in a straight line, and do not miss any of the image.

PRINTING A REPEAT

Before printing a length, a test sample or 'strike-off' should be done to check that the repeat fits together correctly. This can be done on newsprint or cheap cotton fabric. If printing onto newsprint, make sure that it is well taped down so it does not tear or lift away when the screen is moved, especially if there are large, solid areas of print. Number each stop and print *every other* print, ie. print at stops 1, 3, and 5, before going back to fill in the spaces 2, 4, and 6. If you print consecutively, the screen will partially rest on the previous wet print causing it to blur, print paste will also be transferred to the outside of the screen, which will, in turn, transfer onto clean areas of cloth. If printing several colours, it is normally advisable to print the screen with the least coverage first, gradually building up the design, so that drying times are reduced. If combining pigment with dye, the pigment should always be printed first; the cloth will also have to be baked *before* the rest of the print is steamed. It will depend on room temperature, the type of paste being printed together with the fineness of the design, as to whether you can complete all the prints without the screen drying out and blocking. If you are using pigment (especially opaques and metallics), combined with a detailed design, the screen may have to be washed half way through (ie. after 1, 3 and 5). If in any doubt, it is always better to stop and wash the screen rather than continue with a badly printing screen. Keep screens well away from any fan heaters you may be using to dry the print. It is possible to 'flood' the screen by pulling a coat of print paste across with the squeegee, to help prevent drying out. This should be printed off onto newsprint before printing resumes on cloth.

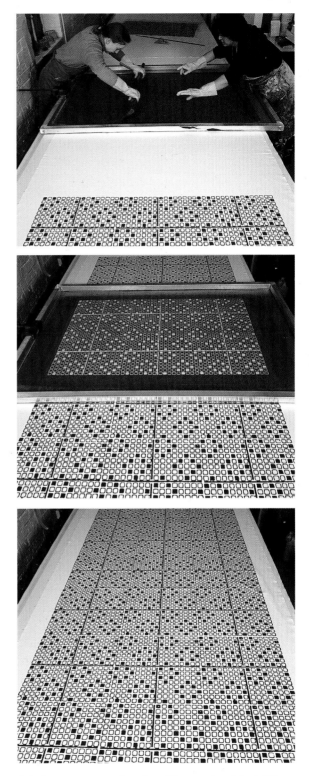

Printing a repeat; prints 1 and 3 are printed first, filling in with 2 once the first two prints are dry. Note the design is printed centrally on the cloth and this is taken into account when positioning the fabric on the table

Fiona McIntosh, 'Tessuti' (UK)
Cubes and cushions; screen-printed discharged cotton – Cubes: 42cm x 42cm x 35cm
Photo: Douglas Robertson

CLEANING A SCREEN AFTER PRINTING

Squeegees and screens should always be washed immediately after printing, especially if pigment is used, which if left to dry can block the mesh and be very difficult to remove.

Use cold water and a hose with reasonable pressure to wash the *inside* of the screen only, making sure that all paste is removed from the edges of the frame. Do not use the hose on the outside of the screen as it can weaken the gummed tape and

damage the emulsion where a detailed image was only given a short exposure time. If printing with deep colours, it can be helpful to lightly sponge the mesh (on the inside) with a weak detergent solution to expel excess dye, after the initial wash, before rinsing thoroughly and gently wiping over mesh and frame with a clean damp cloth. This helps prevent dye bleeding into mesh as the screen dries, and subsequently transferring onto the next print. If there is any paste on the outside of the screen, again gently wipe with a damp cloth. Hold up to the light to check mesh is clear. Ensure that the screen is thoroughly dry before re-use; check there are no small pools of water in the corners or between the mesh and frame, and that the gummed tape is not damp.

CHAPTER TWELVE

FIXING AND FINISHING

FIXING

Fixing a print can be the most important part of the whole printing process, as work can be ruined by incorrect or incomplete fixation. There are various methods of fixation – steaming: saturated, superheated, dry or wet – in this book, only saturated steam is discussed and this is done either at atmospheric pressure or under artificial pressure (pressurised steaming); dry heat (baking/curing); air fixing and wet development.

Exact fixation times for each process will vary depending on the type of equipment used, and it is always advisable to do a test sample first. For the most accurate results, sample conditions should be replicated for a larger piece.

STEAMING

Steaming provides the moisture and heat needed to penetrate the printed cloth, allowing dye to be absorbed into the fibres. Saturated steam is steam which is at the same temperature as, and in the presence of, the water from which it was evaporated. There is always a direct relationship between the temperature and pressure. For example, steam created by boiling water at atmospheric pressure has a temperature of 100°C (212°F), and steam evaporated under a pressure of 10 pounds

has a temperature of 115°C (239°F). Most dyes and fabrics are suitable for fixation by 'saturated steaming at atmospheric pressure'. Some techniques will require the extra heat generated by 'pressure steaming'. Ideal steaming conditions should contain no suspended water droplets and be as air-free as possible.

The main requirement is to protect the printed cloth from direct contact with water, which can cause bleeding, whilst also allowing adequate steam penetration. Cloth (known as a backing cloth) or paper is used to wrap the fabric and this 'parcel' is normally suspended or placed on a rack. The method of wrapping cloth will depend on the type of steamer used. Always remember to replicate steaming conditions from sample to final length, otherwise results will not be consistent.

Steaming can be carried out using a variety of equipment. For small-scale work, a wok or Chinese basket steamer are effective, while a domestic pressure cooker can be used for dyes that require fixation by pressurised steam. By adding the valve weights, the corresponding rise of temperature with pressure is as follows:

pressure:	temperature:
5lbs (2.27kg)	226°F (108°C)
10lbs (4.5kg)	239°F (115°C)
15lbs (6.8kg)	252°F (122°C)

Widely used in the USA and Australia, the horizontal 'stove top' or 'box' steamer is a good, medium-sized, affordable steamer capable of taking cloth up to about 90cm (30″) wide and is suitable for studio use. Made of stainless steel, with a hinged lid, the cloth is rolled onto a rod, which is suspended above the water, and heated by an external heat source.

A vertical 'bullet' steamer will plug into an ordinary domestic (UK) 240V socket. Of double-walled construction with an electric immersion heater, the cylindrical steamer is in two sections for easy handling and can accommodate fabrics up to about 137cm (54″) wide. The cloth is rolled onto a cardboard or plastic tube and is virtually guaranteed drip-free, as water droplets fall directly back down between the two walls into the water reservoir at the bottom. These models usually have a safety cut-out switch.

Other professional steamers capable of holding larger quantities of cloth include star and larger vertical box type steamers. These can steam at either atmospheric pressure or may be designed for pressure steaming. They are very much more expensive and only to be considered for a constant, large output of printing.

A 'dustbin' type steamer is a very economical option, ideal for samples (as it is so quick) and also capable of steaming a reasonably large amount of cloth, which you can easily make yourself – see Chapter 2.

Steaming in a 'bullet' steamer. Here the cloth has been sandwiched between newsprint, rolled onto a cardboard tube and then secured with tape. As with other methods of wrapping for steaming, the cloth should not be rolled too tightly or too loose.

Wrapping fabric and steaming in a dustbin steamer (saturated steaming at atmospheric pressure)

The following describes a procedure I have used for many years steaming in a home-made dustbin steamer, where the cloth is wrapped in a backing cloth and suspended from hooks attached to the lid of the bin. The dustbin itself sits on top of a 'Burco' boiler. The steam generated is intense and very effective. It is possible to steam up to about 6m of a heavy cloth like cotton velvet using this method. Information on making a dustbin steamer and detail on backing cloths is given in Chapter 2. The following is based on a 'Burco' boiler (26 litre boiling capacity) with a diameter of 35cm (13in.), used in conjunction with a 46cm (18in.) diameter galvanised dustbin.

The 'Burco' boiler is filled about one third full with water and switched on to boil, with the dustbin (with lid on) sitting on top. The boiler should take about 30 minutes to reach the required temperature; when steam seeps out from under the dustbin lid, the steamer is hot enough.

1 While the steamer is heating up, lay out a clean, thick backing cloth (not less than 7½oz, but not more than 10oz in weight) that measures no more than about 1.38m (54in.) wide and is 1.5–2m (59-78in.) longer than the printed cloth, on the print table.

2 Position the cloth centrally (width and lengthways), print side down onto the backing cloth and pin to backing at about 30cm (12in.) intervals, along the selvedge edges, also putting a couple of pins in at each end.

3 Lay out double sheets of broadsheet size newspaper horizontally, down the full length of the cloth along the side nearest to you. Position it so that the top edge is just below the centre line of the width of cloth, and the bottom parallel to the selvedge. Overlap each double sheet thickness sheet by a full page, so that there is a total of two layers of newspaper. If the print is heavily discharged, on fine fabric or is wider than the backing cloth (see below), it is advisable to lay down two or three layers of paper at one time.

NOTES:

- If the printed cloth is wider than the backing cloth, either:

  - for an all-over print: position the cloth 2–3cm in from the edge of the backing cloth along the edge nearest to you and lay a further length of newspaper down parallel to and just below the top edge of the backing cloth (covering the reverse of the printed cloth), so that the excess printed cloth can be folded back over on top of this paper, preventing direct contact of print against print. Carefully pin the fabric and newspaper together at each end of the length, with perhaps two or three extra pins carefully positioned at intervals along the selvedge edge of the fabric to help secure prior to folding

  or

  - if the print is narrower than the cloth it is printed on: position the cloth centrally as before and carefully fold in excess unprinted cloth down each selvedge edge, before proceeding as normal with the newspaper

  - If just steaming small samples:
    Position the fabric samples centrally lengthways and just below the centre fold line of the backing cloth

Remember that with all methods of folding cloth, it is imperative that there is always a layer (or layers) of newspaper between any two layers of printed cloth.

4 The backing cloth and printed fabric are then folded in *half* horizontally (fold 'A'). Lift the half of cloth that *doesn't* have newspaper on, bringing it towards you so that the selvedges

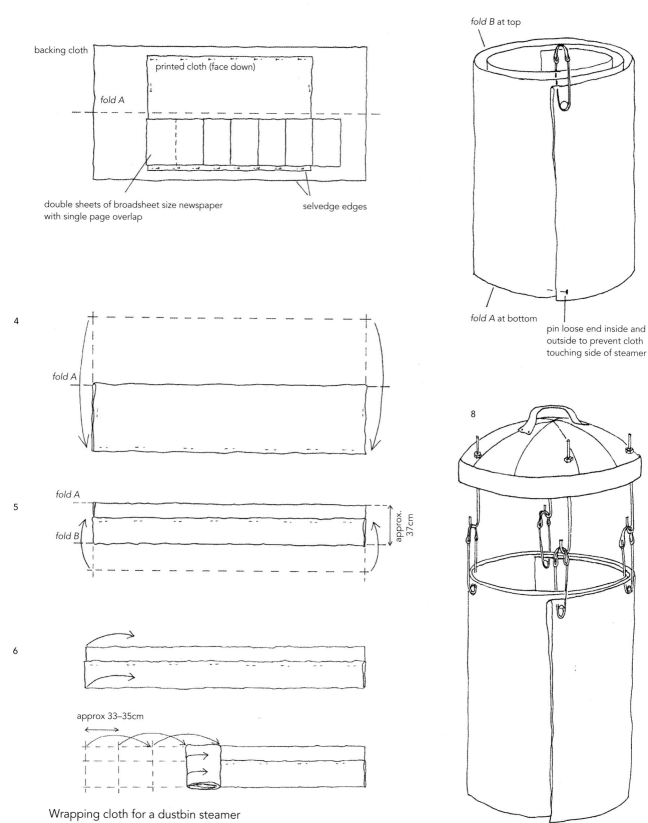

backing cloth

printed cloth (face down)

fold A

double sheets of broadsheet size newspaper
with single page overlap

selvedge edges

4

fold A

5

fold A

fold B

approx.
37cm

6

approx 33–35cm

Wrapping cloth for a dustbin steamer

fold B at top

fold A at bottom

pin loose end inside and
outside to prevent cloth
touching side of steamer

8

of the backing cloth lie on top of each other. If you are steaming cloth that is wider than the backing cloth as outlined above, you will have an extra line of newspaper sandwiched along the top half of the cloth and it is helpful to get someone to help you with this fold, to ensure the newspaper remains in place.

5 Next, again folding lengthways, lift the selvedge edges and fold back to within a few centimetres of the folded edge, or so that the total depth of the cloth is about 37cm (15in.) (fold 'B').

6 Fold over one end at a distance of about 33–35cm (13–14in.) and continue carefully folding all the way along, taking care not to make the parcel too tight or too loose.

7 Stand the 'folded parcel' upright so that the (internally) visible selvedge edges of the backing cloth face downwards. Secure the loose ends (in and outside of the 'parcel') using two kilt pins opposite each other. Pin through each layer of *backing cloth only*, taking care not to go through the printed cloth. Use four evenly spaced pins if the cloth is heavy, to ensure the package is properly supported. Lay the parcel on its side at the edge of a table, with the kilt pins nearest to you.

8 When the steamer is hot enough, carefully lift the lid (wearing gloves) and tilt slightly over the dustbin, so that any moisture that has built-up can run off. Attach the kilt pins to the hooks in the lid while the cloth is in a horizontal position on the table. Raise the lid and cloth to a vertical position, and supporting the underneath if necessary, carefully lower the cloth into the steamer. **The cloth should not touch either the sides or the bottom of the dustbin.** If it touches the sides, the parcel should be re-rolled at slightly smaller intervals. If touching the bottom of the dustbin,

the backing cloth may be too wide or not have been folded correctly. Any direct contact made with the steamer may result in a bleeding print.

9 Steam for the required amount of time. Use an electronic timer, as it is extremely easy to lose track of time when steaming!

10 When steaming is complete, lift the lid high enough so that the cloth clears the steamer, without touching the sides and rest on a heatproof surface *on its side*; this allows any moisture on the lid to run off safely. Release the pins from the hooks, replace the lid and switch the steamer off. Allow the cloth to cool for a few moments only before unwrapping on the table (remember to protect the table surface, as heat can cause discolouration to neoprene). Do not leave cloth in the backing cloth, even if you are not ready to wash it out immediately.

11 For repeated steaming, check that the water is topped up to return to the one-third full level.

NOTES:

- For steaming cloth that requires to be wrapped in a backing cloth wider than 150cm, it may be necessary to fold in a slightly different way to prevent the final cloth 'parcel' from touching the bottom of the dustbin
- Experimentation with steaming times will be **essential**, to ensure full and effective steam penetration on a variety of fabrics of different thicknesses and finishes using different dye types and processes

Calculating increased steaming times for longer lengths

Having completed successful samples, you will want to feel confident in calculating the steaming time for a final length. The best way of assessing this is to steam a final sample in the same size and thickness of backing cloth that will be used for the length. Position the sample face down at *one end* of the backing cloth, and lay an unprinted piece of the same fabric cut to the same size as the final length will be, next to the sample(s). Fold the cloth in the normal way, and start the final rolling of the backing cloth **from the end where the sample is positioned**, so that it ends up being in the middle of the parcel. This is because the centre takes the longest to achieve full steam penetration, whereas cloth that ends up being near to, or on the outside of the parcel will steam more quickly.

Steaming long lengths of cloth

The longer the parcel of backing cloth and fabric, the more densely packed and folded it will be, sometimes resulting in less than even steam penetration, despite the overall steaming time

being correct. For long lengths of some thicker or bulkier fabrics, it may be necessary to remove the backing cloth parcel half way though steaming and re-fold so that the positioning of cloth within the steamer is reversed for the second half of steaming. For example, if the total steaming time is 30 minutes, remove the cloth after 15 minutes (leaving the steamer switched on). Carefully remove the kilt pins and unroll the parcel on the print table, taking note of which

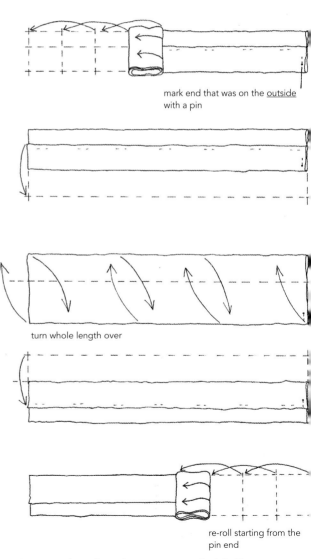

mark end that was on the <u>outside</u> with a pin

turn whole length over

re-roll starting from the pin end

Steaming long lengths – reversing cloth half way through

154

end was *on the outside* of the roll (marking with a pin is helpful). Holding the selvedge edges of the backing cloth, undo the first horizontal fold, so that the backing cloth is just folded in half once. Get someone to stand at one end and help turn the whole thing over, so that the side that was against the table is now the side facing upwards. Re-do the selvedge edge (horizontal) fold as normal and then re-roll, this time *beginning to roll with the end that was previously on the outside* (marked with a pin), so that this will now be in the centre. In this way, all areas of print should receive equal and adequate steam penetration.

DRY HEAT (BAKING OR CURING)

Baking is mainly used for fixing pigments, but can also be used for some reactive dyes as well as baking acid devoré prints . On a large scale, cloth may be hung in a baking cabinet or cured horizontally on a conveyor belt, which passes underneath the heat source. For a studio set-up, smaller sample machines are more feasible, along with some infra-red heating units, which are capable of reaching the high temperatures required. Samples can be ironed for about 5 minutes on the reverse (do on a backing cloth) using a hot iron set at cotton. For synthetics, iron at a lower temperature for longer or put in a tumble dryer on the highest setting for up to 30 minutes. A heat press can also be used for fixing small-scale work.

AIR FIXING

Cloth dyed with vat dyes may be fixed by hanging in the air for up to 24 hours, to achieve full oxidisation. The very reactive cold water dyes (like Procion MX) can also be fixed in this way, although it is not as effective as steaming.

WET DEVELOPMENT

This is an alternative method for developing and fixing cloth dyed with vat dyes (see recipe). The cloth is treated in a bath containing a suitable oxidising agent, which stimulates full colour development. It is also used with some other dye systems and for resist techniques like batik.

Joanna Kinnersly-
Taylor (UK)
'Red Glasshouse', 1998
Dyed, screen-printed and
hand-painted linen union
using reactive dyes and
discharge,
75cm x 40cm x 2.3cm

STEAMING PROBLEMS

Symptom	Possible cause & solution
Print washes out completely	• Cloth inadequately prepared; needs further scouring • Check dye type compatible for cloth • Check all relevant auxiliaries added to print paste • Check print paste fresh (generally not over one month old) • Too short a steaming time • Too much time has elapsed between printing and steaming
Print partially washes out leaving an even, faded impression	• Cloth inadequately prepared; needs further scouring • Print paste out of date • Too short a steaming time • Too much time has elapsed between printing and steaming
Print is clear in some areas, faded in others	• Backing cloth rolled too tightly • Backing cloth is bulky and needs to be re-rolled half way through steaming to re-distribute printed cloth
In a mixed print, discharge has steamed correctly but underlying print washes out or fades	• Steaming time is too short for print paste, although adequate for discharge
Discharge does not react as expected	• Check discharge fresh and of correct strength • Not enough pulls • Too short/long a steaming time
Colours have changed completely	• Too long a steaming time

Print has bled in places	• Print has come into direct contact with moisture:
	  i) check backing cloth is not touching the sides or bottom of steamer or
	  ii) that dripping has not occurred from lid during insertion/removal from steamer or
	  iii) that kilt pin has not been inserted through fabric with moisture transferral during removal after steaming
	• The print was not completely dry prior to steaming

The print has bled evenly	• The print was not completely dry prior to steaming • There is too much humectant in the print paste (ie. urea) • Too long a steaming time for that particular fabric
There are holes in the cloth	• The kilt pins have gone through the printed cloth instead of just the backing cloth

This is generally done in three stages; chiefly, cold until clear; warm or hot with a neutral detergent for a few minutes; cold until clear. There are variations for different dye groups, processes and fabrics. It is very important to remove all excess dyestuff, discharge and paste residue from cloth, otherwise colours can run or bleed or spoil subsequent processes. Use the largest vessel possible to wash out in, filling with water and agitating the cloth vigorously, before refilling with fresh water. Have a glass jug handy to scoop out rinsing water and monitor the progress of dye removal. Pale colours will normally wash out quite quickly, but full strength pastes on very absorbent cloth will take much longer. Discharge prints over previously unfixed dye may leave a residue which can be removed with a nailbrush.

Spin cloth well after the final rinse. Do not leave damp cloth in a spin dryer or laundry basket; always hang up to dry straight away. With some fabrics it may be preferable to iron whilst damp on a clean backing cloth. Some fabrics may stretch at this stage, especially linen, and it can be helpful to tumble dry for a very short period, before ironing dry, to aid registration if overprinting.

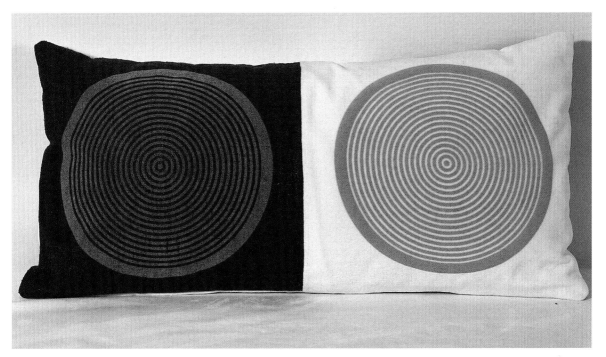

Double Helix (UK)
Cushion, flock printed on natural silk and velvet
Photo: Ruth Clark

LIST OF AUXILIARIES AND THEIR FUNCTIONS

Acetic acid

Assists dye bond and promotes dye exhaustion in acid dye-baths. Also used in penultimate rinse for silk, to restore lustre, and in oxidising baths for vat dye prints.

Buy at 100% and mix to a safe working strength of 20% (1 part acid to 4 parts water). Wearing goggles and gloves, add 200ml acetic acid *very slowly* to 800ml cold water to avoid rising fumes (not the other way round), stirring gently, to make 1 litre of dilute acid. Alternatively, use ordinary white malt vinegar, which has a strength of about 4%. You will therefore need to use five times the amount of vinegar to that of acetic acid stated in the recipe, to achieve the desired strength. Catering sized bottles of acetic acid (80%) or white malt vinegar can be obtained from food wholesalers.

NOTE:
In the USA, acetic acid comes in a weaker 56% strength, (about 11 times stronger than household vinegar of 5%), so adjust the dilution quantity accordingly to make a 20% strength solution. Add 350ml acetic acid *very slowly* to 630ml cold water.
See also citric acid.

Acidic salts

These are mild acids in dry form and are suitable for dye-baths that do not need a strong acid. Their addition assists in achieving level dyeing by acidifying the dye-bath gradually as the temperature increases. Some salts are also used for the 'wet development' stage. They can either be used dry or made into a solution of a known strength, which makes it easier to measure a small quantity. To make a 10% solution, dissolve 10g of acidic salt in 100ml boiling water.

Alum

See potassium aluminium sulphate.

Aluminium sulphate

Acid used to destroy cellulose fibres in devoré paste.

Ammonium acetate

Acidic salt used in acid dye-baths to promote gradual, even dyeing. In solution, used in the 'wet development' stage of colour discharge on silk, wool and nylon.

Ammonium oxalate

Acid donor in print pastes enabling dye fixation, especially on silk and nylon.

Ammonium sulphate

Acidic salt used in acid dye-baths to promote gradual, even dyeing. Can also be used as an acid donor in print pastes enabling dye fixation but may cause yellowing. In solution, they are used in the 'wet development' stage of colour discharge on silk, wool and nylon. For measuring small quantities for sample dyeing, it may be easier to make up a 10% solution. Dissolve 10g of the dry salts in 100ml boiling water, or 100g in 1000ml water and so on, retaining the ratio; this means that 1g of ammonium sulphate will be present in every 10ml of solution.

Ammonium tartrate

Acid donor in print pastes enabling dye fixation, especially on silk and nylon.

Anthraquinone powder

This yellow crystalline compound is the basis of many natural and synthetic dyes and is obtained by oxidisation of anthracene. Anthracene itself is a colourless crystalline hydrocarbon formed by distillation of crude oils. Anthraquinone powder helps improve the clarity of colour discharge using reactive, direct or vat dyes as illuminants.

Baking soda

See sodium bicarbonate.

Caustic soda

See sodium hydroxide.

Citric acid

May be substituted for acetic acid in equal measure; no sour smell is given off during the dyeing process. Citric acid crystals may also be used in the following quantity:

1 teaspoon crystals = 1 teaspoon acetic acid 56% strength (USA)

Common salt

See sodium chloride.

Dextrin (British gum)

A soluble gummy substance obtained by hydrolysis of starch; used in thickeners and resist pastes.

Disodium hydrogen phosphate

An acid donor which may be used in direct dye print paste to reduce alkalinity slightly in a hard water area, especially when printing on wool. Also in disperse dye paste when printing on polyester, enabling dye fixation. Compatible with alginate gums.

Ethoxylated alcohol

Used to paste certain dyes to aid dissolution.

Glauber's salt

See sodium sulphate.

Glycerine / Glycerol

Solvent and hygroscopic agent used to dissolve certain dyestuffs.

Hydrogen peroxide

An oxidizing agent used at the 'wet development' stage of certain dyestuffs, also used in an acid bleaching bath for protein fibres. Buy at 30% ('100 volumes') and dilute to make a working strength of 6% by mixing 1 part hydrogen peroxide to 4 parts water.

Lye

See sodium hydroxide.

Potassium aluminium sulphate (alum)

Mordant. Used in this book in the flour resist paste.

Potassium carbonate (pot ash)

Alkali that can be used in vat dye print paste in place of sodium carbonate.

Soda ash

See sodium carbonate.

Sodium acetate

Acid forming salt. Acts as a levelling agent for certain dye-stuffs.

Sodium alginate

Found in many brown seaweeds, the basis of thickeners for a variety of dye types.

e.g.: 'Manutex F' (high solids content) (UK/AUS) is equivalent to Sodium Alginate 'F' or 'L' (USA) 'Manutex RS' (low solids content) (UK/AUS) is equivalent to Sodium Alginate 'SH' or 'H' (USA)

Sodium bicarbonate (baking soda)

Weak alkali used in reactive dye print paste to promote the chemical reaction between dye and fibre, enabling fixation.

Sodium bisulphate

Crystals that form a very strong acid when dissolved in water.

Sodium bisulphite

May be used with reactive cold water dyes to increase dye absorption when dyeing protein fibres or nylon. 'Anti-Chlor' concentrate (USA) is a *sodium bisulphite compound* which neutralises residual chlorine when removing colour with hypochlorite bleach and prevents cloth disintegration.

Sodium carbonate (soda ash)

Alkali used for dyeing cellulose fibres, promoting the chemical reaction between dye and fibre, enabling fixation; also for scouring fabrics.

Sodium chloride (common salt)

Aids dye absorption and levelling in the dye-bath.

Sodium chlorite

Bleaching agent.

Sodium dithionite

See sodium hydrogen sulphite.

Sodium formaldehyde sulphoxylate

A reducing agent used in discharge paste on cellulose, viscose rayon, cellulose acetate and tri-acetate and also on silk, requiring alkali conditions,

e.g.: 'Formosul' (UK & USA)

Sodium hexametaphosphate

Used in water softeners.

e.g.: 'Calgon' (UK/USA)
'Metaphos' (pure form with no additives) (USA)

Sodium hydrogen sulphate (hydrosulphate)

Acid used to destroy cellulose fibres in devoré paste.

Sodium hydrogen sulphite (hydrosulphite) or dithionite

Also see thiurea dioxide. Used in vat dyeing to 'reduce' the dye, also for stripping dyed cloth.

Sodium hydroxide (caustic soda)
(sometimes referred to as lye in USA)

Alkali used to destroy protein fibres in devoré paste; also used in vat dyeing and in crimping. For ease, this can be made to a standard strength by dissolving 441g sodium hydroxide (comes in flakes, granules or pellets) in 1 litre cold water. The viscosity should be checked with a hydrometer before use.

Sodium hypochlorite

Used in bleaching baths for cellulose fibres. Ordinary domestic bleach contains about 4% sodium hypochlorite

Sodium salt of m-nitrobenzene sulphonic acid

A mild oxidising agent that prevents reduction of reactive (H) dyes during fixation, to produce brighter colours.

e.g.: 'Ludigol' / 'Ludigol F' (USA)
'Chem Flakes' (USA)

Sodium silicate

Alkali used in bleaching bath for wool and silk and for scouring heavyweight linen.

Sodium sulphate (Glauber's salt)

Retards dye take-up to aid level dyeing.

Tannic acid

A mordant.

Thiurea dioxide

Reducing agent for use on nylon. As a safe replacement for sodium hydrogen sulphite (hydrosulphite) or dithionite, it can also be used in vat dyeing and for stripping dyed cloth. It is five times stronger, non-flammable and has a good shelf life. Do not use with aluminium, cast iron or copper vessels and utensils.

e.g.: 'Manofast' (UK)
'Thiox' (USA)

Urea

Colourless crystalline compound of ammonia and carbon dioxide. Hygroscopic agent used to assist dissolution of dyes. Humecant in printing and painting all dye types.

Washing soda crystals

An impure form of sodium carbonate, and half the strength, but may be used as an alkali for dyeing cellulose fibres, promoting the chemical reaction between dye and fibre, enabling fixation; also for scouring fabrics.

Zinc formaldehyde desulphoxylate

A reducing agent requiring acidic conditions used in discharge paste on silk, wool, synthetics and with pigments on cellulose. e.g.: 'Decrolin' (UK)

GLOSSARY

Acid donor

Acidic substances used in certain print pastes to enable dye fixation.

Acid dyes

Divided into three main categories: levelling, milling and metal-complex, these dyes have a natural affinity for protein fibres and can also be used to dye nylon.

Alginates

Term used to describe thickeners made from sodium alginate, which is found in many brown seaweeds. 'Manutex' is the proprietary brand of sodium alginate.

Auxiliary

A chemical assistant which enables the processes in dyeing and printing to be carried out effectively.

Bain-marie

Double boiler; a vessel of hot water, into which another container is placed for slow and gentle heating.

Basic dyes

The oldest type of synthetic dye. Although the colours are brilliant, these dyes are unstable and consequently wash and lightfast properties are very poor. Basic dyes are also known to be carcinogenic.

Baumé – abbreviated to °Bé

Scale of specific gravity or density of liquids.

Binder

Another word for thickener, used especially with pigment pastes.

Carrier

A substance used to support or convey another substance, e.g. to promote a dye bond with hydrophobic synthetic fibres in a disperse dye-bath.

Cellulose ether

Formed by etherification of cellulose to produce a soluble substance used as a thickener that is capable of withstanding acidic conditions.

Cyanotype (Blueprint)

A simple, historic photographic process that can be used to create images directly onto cloth (natural fibres only).

Devoré

A technique which involves burning away or destroying one or more of the fibres in a mixed fibre cloth. This is achieved by the application of a caustic paste (usually screen-printed) and subsequent exposure to heat by baking.

Direct dyes

An older class of dye developed for use specifically on cellulose fibres without requiring the assistance of a mordant.

Disperse dyes

Designed specifically for man-made, often hydrophobic fibres such as polyester and acetates. As they do not dissolve in water, disperse dyes need to be applied with the aid of a dispersing agent; a carrier may also be required, especially with polyester.

Dispersing agent

Aids even distribution of dye particles in the dye-bath, especially with disperse dyes.

Dye-bath

Used to describe the vessel (and its contents) in which fabric is dyed.

Dye-bath assistant

An auxiliary ingredient required in the dye-bath to carry out the dyeing process effectively.

Dye liquor

Solution of dissolved dyestuff prior to its addition to dye-bath or print paste.

Fixing agent

For optional use at washing-out stage of prints to help prevent bleeding of dyestuffs, especially useful with direct dyes.

e.g.: 'Fixitol P' (UK)
       'Raycafix' (USA)

Frottage

The technique of taking a rubbing from an uneven surface.

Humectant

A moisture retaining substance; urea is a humectant.

Hydrometer

A simple calibrated instrument for measuring gravity or density of liquids.

Hydrophobic

A substance which tends to repel or fails to mix with water.

Hygroscopic

A substance which tends to absorb moisture from the air.

Illuminating dye

A dye which is suitable for use in colour discharge printing. A good illuminating dye will have *poor* dischargeability (ie. be very fast), so that it withstands the effects of the reducing agent.

Levelling agent

A surfactant which may be added to the dye-bath to restrict the rate at which dye is absorbed, helping to promote even or 'level' dyeing.

Liquor ratio

In a dye-bath, the proportion of water to the weight of cloth.

Metal-complex dyes

These fall within the acid dye group, having a natural affinity for protein fibres without the need for a mordant. They are divided into two types: 1:1 (1 metal atom to 1 dye molecule) and 1:2 (1 metal atom to 2 dye molecules).

Modified starch

As a starch ether, modified starch can withstand strong alkaline conditions without breaking down, and is used in gums for discharge printing.

e.g.: 'Solvitose C5' (UK)
       'Monagum' (USA)

Moiré

A pattern of irregular wavy lines caused by the superimposition of two sets of closely spaced lines.

Mordant

Mordants are chemical assistants, mostly made from metal salts, alum being the most commonly used. Applied in solution to the cloth, they assist dye fixation. Most natural dyes require a mordant.

Oxidize

To cause to combine chemically with oxygen. To undergo a reaction in which electrons are *lost* to another substance; the opposite of reduce.

Oxidizing agent

A substance that withdraws hydrogen from, or adds oxygen to another substance; the opposite of a reducing agent. In printing, an oxidizing agent is used in the print paste to prevent decomposition of the dye and aiding its absorption and fixation on the cloth.

e.g.: 'Matexil P-AL' (UK)
       'Ludigol' / 'Ludigol F' (USA)
       'Chem Flakes' (USA)

pH value

A figure indicating the acidity or alkalinity of a solution on a logarithmic scale, where 7 is neutral, numbers below 7 are more acid and numbers above more alkaline. The pH value measures the level of hydrogen ion concentration.

pH neutral detergent

A fine, concentrated, neutral detergent, used in the hot wash after dyeing or steaming prints.

e.g.: 'Metapex 26' (UK)

'Synthrapol SP' or 'Synthrapol LF' (USA)

'Mesitol NBS' (AUS)

Photogram

A image produced with photographic materials, such as light sensitive paper, but without a camera.

Pressurised steaming

Saturated steam generated under artificial pressure is hotter than that created at atmospheric pressure. Fixation of some dye-stuffs is only possible under these conditions.

p.s.i.

Pounds per square inch. Used as measurement of pressure.

Reactive dyes

These dyes react directly with the fibre, and when chemically fixed in an alkaline environment, produce a permanent bond. This results in excellent washing and lightfastness properties.

Reduce

To cause to combine chemically with hydrogen. To undergo a reaction in which electrons are *gained* from another substance; the opposite of oxidize.

Reducing agent

A substance that withdraws oxygen from, or adds hydrogen to another substance; the opposite of oxidizing agent. In discharge printing, the use of a reducing agent results in colour removal during steaming.

e.g.: 'Decrolin' (UK)

'Formosul' (UK & USA)

'Thiox' (USA)

Saturated steaming

Steam which is at the same temperature as, and in the presence of, the water from which it was evaporated.

Slurry

A semi-liquid mixture.

Starch ether

Formed by etherification of a starch to produce a dissolvable substance used as a thickener capable of withstanding strong alkaline conditions.

e.g.: 'Solvitose C5' (UK)

'Monagum' (USA)

Substantivity

The affinity between a substrate and a dye or other chemical applied to it. A mordant is not required.

Substrate

The base cloth or fabric to which dyes and chemicals can be applied.

Surfactant

A substance which reduces the surface tension of a liquid in which it is dissolved. Surfactants can be used as wetting-out and levelling agents.

e.g.: 'Synthrapol SP' / 'Synthrapol LF' (low foaming) (USA)

'Synthrapol' may also be used as a pre-wash and as an afterwash.

'Wetter CDE' (AUS)

Thickener

A thickener forms the basis of all print pastes, and is the vehicle for the other printing auxiliaries and dyestuffs which are added to it.

Twaddell – abbreviated to ° Tw

Scale of specific gravity or density of liquids.

Vat dyes

These dyes are insoluble and have to be 'reduced' in the dye-bath in order to transfer to the cloth. The dye is then fixed to the fibres through oxidisation where it returns to its insoluble form. Suitable for cellulose fibres, with excellent light and washfastness properties.

Vortex

A mass of whirling fluid.

Wet development

This is an alternative method for developing and fixing cloth dyed with vat dyes, some other dye systems and for resist techniques like batik. The cloth is treated in a bath containing a suitable oxidising agent, which stimulates full colour development.

Wetting-out

The process in which cloth is thoroughly saturated with the water in the dye-bath prior to the addition of the dye.

Wetting-out agent

A surfactant that may be used as an addition to the dye-bath, to assist wetting-out and subsequent dye absorption on certain fabrics, especially those that are tightly woven.

e.g.:   'Matexil WA-KBN' (UK)
         'Calsolene' (USA)

Whitener

Zinc oxide or titanium oxide are whiteners which may be used in Decrolin discharge pastes to improve whiteness.

Sally Greaves-Lord (UK)
'Glowing Embers', 2000
Hand-painted with acid dyes
and dicharge on silk;
92cm x 180cm
Photo; Steve Yates

CONVERSION CHARTS

CAPACITY

litres	US gallons	& pints	US gallons	litres
1		2.11	1	3.7853
2		4.23	2	7.5706
3		6.34	3	11.3559
4	1	0.45	4	15.1412
5	1	2.56	5	18.9265
6	1	4.68	6	22.7118
7	1	6.79	7	26.4971
8	2	0.91	8	30.2824
9	2	3.02	9	34.0677
10	2	5.13	10	37.853
15	3	7.70	20	75.706
20	5	2.27	30	113.559
25	6	4.83	40	151.412
50	13	1.66	50	189.265

LENGTH

Centimetres	Inches
1	.394
2	.79
3	1.18
4	1.575
5	1.97
6	2.36
7	2.756
8	3.15
9	3.546
10	3.94
50	19.69
100	39.37

to convert from inches to centimetres:
multiply by 2.54

Feet	Metres	Yards
3.28	1	1.094
6.56	2	2.187
9.84	3	3.28
13.12	4	4.375
16.4	5	5.47
19.69	6	6.56
22.97	7	7.66
26.25	8	8.75
29.53	9	9.84
32.81	10	10.94

to convert from feet to metres:
multiply by 0.3048
to convert from yards to metres:
multiply by 0.9144

WEIGHT

Metric (grams/ kilograms)	Imperial (ounces/ pounds)
1	0.035
2	0.07
3	0.11
4	0.14
5	0.18
6	0.21
7	0.25
8	0.28
9	0.32
10	0.35
15	0.53
20	0.71
25	0.88
50	1.76
100	3.5
500	1.15lbs
1000 (1kg)	2.2lbs

TEMPERATURE

Celsius °C	Fahrenheit °F
30	86
35	95
40	104
45	113
50	122
55	131
60	140
65	149
70	158
75	167
80	176
85	185
90	194
95	203
100	212
110	230
120	248
130	266
140	284
150	302
160	320
170	338
180	356
190	374
200	392

To convert from Celsius to Fahrenheit:
$F = (9/5 \times Celsius) + 32$
To convert from Fahrenheit to Celsius:
$C = 5/9 \times (Fahrenheit - 32)$

INTERNATIONAL PAPER SIZES

THE A SERIES

Size	Millimetres	Inches
A0	841 x 1189	$33\frac{1}{8}$ x $46\frac{3}{4}$
A1	594 x 841	$23\frac{3}{8}$ x $33\frac{1}{8}$
A2	420 x 594	$16\frac{1}{2}$ x $23\frac{3}{8}$
A3	297 x 420	$11\frac{3}{4}$ x $16\frac{1}{2}$
A4	210 x 297	$8\frac{1}{4}$ x $11\frac{3}{4}$
A5	148 x 210	$5\frac{7}{8}$ x $8\frac{1}{4}$
A6	105 x 148	$4\frac{1}{8}$ x $5\frac{7}{8}$
A7	74 x 105	$2\frac{7}{8}$ x $4\frac{1}{8}$

ADDRESS LIST

UK

Suppliers

ABC Chemical Company Ltd
Castle Hill
Todmorden
Lancashire OL14 5TD
TEL: (01706) 818800
FAX: (01706) 819554
table gum

Adelco Screen Process Ltd
Highview
High Street
Bordon
Hampshire GU35 0AX
TEL: (01420) 488388
FAX: (01420) 476445
E-MAIL: sales@adelco.co.uk
www.adelco.co.uk
screen-printing equipment and services

ARCO Ltd (head office)
PO Box 21
Waverley Street
Hull HU1 2SJ
TEL: (01482) 222522
FAX: (01482) 218536
E-MAIL: sales@arco.co.uk
www.arco.co.uk
branches UK-wide
personal protection equipment including fume/dust masks

NES Arnold
Novara House
Excelsior Road
Ashby Park
Ashby-de-la-Zouch
Leicestershire LE65 1NG
TEL: (0870) 6000 192
FAX: (0800) 328 0001
rolls of newsprint

Ashill Colour Studio
Boundary Cottage
172 Clifton Road
Shefford
Bedfordshire SG17 5AH
TEL: (01462) 812001
CONTACT: Jenny Dean
natural dyes and mordants, books

BASF plc
PO Box 4
Earl Road
Cheadle Hulme
Cheshire SK8 6QG
TEL: (0161) 485 6222
FAX: (0161) 486 0891
www.basf-plc.co.uk
dyeing and printing auxiliaries, pigments

Bayer plc
Greenside Way
Chadderton Industrial Estate
Greengate, Middleton
Manchester M24 1SW
TEL: (0161) 682 1589
FAX: (0161) 684 9147
www.bayertextile.com
pigments and auxiliaries

Burco Dean Appliances Ltd
Langham Street
Rosegrove
Burnley
Lancashire
BB12 6AL
TEL: (01282) 427241
www.burcodean.com
Burco catering urns and washboilers (for steaming)

Candlemakers Supplies
28 Blythe Road
Olympia
London W14 0HA
TEL: (020) 7602 4031/2
FAX: (020) 7602 2796
www.candlemakers.co.uk
reactive dyes, batik equipment, fabric inks and paints

Ciba Specialty Chemicals plc
Charter Way
Macclesfield
Cheshire
SK10 2NX
TEL: (01625) 421933
www.cibasc.com
dyes and auxiliaries

Clariant
Calverley Lane
Horsforth
Leeds LS18 4RP
TEL: (0113) 258 4646
FAX: (0113) 259 1632
www.clariant.com
dyes and auxiliaries

Dylon International Ltd
Worsley Bridge Road
Lower Sydenham
London SE26 5HD
TEL: (020) 8663 4801
FAX: (020) 8658 6735
www.dylon.co.uk
Dylon multi-purpose and reactive dyes, chemicals

HSE
Health & Safety Executive
Information Centre
Broad Lane
Sheffield S3 7HQ
HSE InfoLine:
(0541) 545500
health and safety information

Kemtex Educational Supplies
Chorley Business & Technology
Centre
Euxton Lane
Chorley
Lancashire PR7 6TE
TEL: (01257) 230220
FAX: (01257) 230225
CONTACT: Peter Leadbetter
www.kemtex.co.uk
www.textiledyes.co.uk
*dyes and auxiliaries sold in smaller
quantities, syringes and beakers;
very helpful service*

London Screen Service
Unit 75, Parkside Business Estate
Blackhorse Road
London SE8 5HZ
TEL: (020) 8694 9717
FAX: (020) 8694 9423
CONTACT: Andy Leggatt
*screen-printing equipment including
screens, screen mesh, squeegees,
coating troughs, chemicals, screen
re-stretching; very helpful service*

MacCulloch and Wallis Ltd
25 Dering Street
London W1R 0BH
TEL: (020) 7409 0725
FAX: (020) 7491 2481
www.macculloch-wallis.co.uk
*dress fabrics, silks, interlinings,
haberdashery, sewing equipment*

Magna Colours Ltd
Dodworth Business Park
Upper Cliffe Road
Dodworth
Barnsley
South Yorkshire S75 3SP
TEL: (01226) 731751
FAX: (01226) 731752
www.magnacolours.com
*excellent range of pigments and
binders*

Merck Eurolab
Merck House
Poole
Dorset BH15 1TD
TEL: (01202) 669700
FAX: (01202) 665599
www.bdh.com
chemicals, precision scales

Midland Dykem Ltd
71 Paget Road
Leicester LE3 5HN
TEL: (0116) 262 4975
FAX: (0116) 262 7425
E-MAIL: bargains@midland
dykem.com
www.midlanddykem.com
*extensive budget range of dyes (ex-
stock, tested prior to despatch; larger
quantities only), pigments &
auxiliaries, dyehouse equipment
including stainless steel jugs, utensils
and containers*

Ohaus UK Ltd
64 Boston Road
Beaumont Leys
Leicester LE4 1AW
TEL: (0116) 2345075
www.ohaus.com
wide range of precision scales

Pongees Ltd
28–30 Hoxton Square
London N1 6NN
TEL: (020) 7739 9130
FAX: (020) 7739 9132
E-MAIL: info@pongees.co.uk
www.pongees.co.uk
wide range of silks

John Purcell Paper
15 Rumsey Road
London SW9 0TR
TEL: (020) 7737 5199
FAX: (020) 7737 6765
*'True-Grain' textured polyester
drawing film*

Quality Colours (London) Ltd
Unit 13
Gemini Project
Landmann Way
London SE14 5RL
TEL: (020) 7394 8775
FAX: (020) 7237 1044
CONTACT: Peter Wilkes
www.qualitycolours.co.uk
*excellent range of dyes, pigments,
binders and chemicals, all sold in
smaller quantities; also containers
very helpful service*

Scientific & Chemical Supplies Ltd
Carlton House
Livingstone Road
Bilston
West Midlands WW14 0QZ
TEL: (01902) 402402
FAX: (01902) 402343
E-MAIL: scs@scichem.co.uk
www.scichem.co.uk
*chemicals, safety equipment,
laboratory supplies*

Scientific Laboratory Supplies
Wilford Industrial Estate
Ruddington Lane
Wilford
Nottinghamshire NG11 7EP
TEL: (0115) 982 1111
www.scientific-labs.com
*'Tri-pour' beakers (minimum order
value £25)*

Screenchem Products Ltd
5 Telford Place
East Lenzie Mill
Cumbernauld
Glasgow G67 2NH
TEL: (01236) 733276
*Ulano emulsion, coating troughs,
screens and screen re-stretching
service, squeegees and larger printing
equipment*

Selectasine Serigraphics Ltd
65 Chislehurst Road
Chislehurst
Kent BR7 5NP
TEL: (020) 8467 8544
FAX: (020) 8295 0808
*pigments and binders, screen mesh,
'Profilm' stencil, drafting film, film,
newsprint, emulsion, screens,
squeegees*

Sericol Ltd (head office)
Pysons Road
Broadstairs
Kent BT10 2LE
TEL: (01843) 866668
FAX: (01843) 872074
technical helpline: (08457)708070
UK sales: (01992) 782619
UK sales FAX: (01992) 782602
www.sericol.co.uk
*wide range of screen-printing
supplies including drafting film
('Seritrace')*

Slidepacks
16 Templemead Close
Stanmore
Middlesex HA7 3RG
TEL: (020) 8954 7048
FAX: (020) 8954 1110
E-MAIL: sales@slidepacks.com
www.slidepacks.com
*archival quality photographic
storage sheets (eg. for slides and
6" x 4" photo sheets for fabric
samples)*

R A Smart (Holdings) Ltd
Clough Bank
Grimshaw Lane
Bollington
Macclesfield
Cheshire SK10 5NZ
TEL: (01625) 576231
FAX: (01625) 576201
CONTACT: Magnus Mighall
www. RASmart.co.uk
*wide range of screen printing
equipment including print tables,
exposure units and steamers*

Suasion Ltd
The Studio
1 Stevenage Road
Knebworth
Herts SG3 6AN
TEL/FAX: (01438) 815252
E-MAIL: suasion@aol.com
www.suasion-uk.com
*UK distributors of the Jacquard
(USA) range of dyes and auxiliaries;
also screens and screen mesh,
squeegees and Huntspeedball screen
emulsion and sensitiser, screen-
printing workshops*

Tiranti
27 Warren Street
London W1P 5DG
TEL/FAX: (020) 7636 8565
www.tiranti.co.uk
latex, measuring bottles

George Weil and Fibrecrafts
1 Old Portsmouth Road
Peasmarsh
Guildford
Surrey GU3 1LZ
TEL: (01483) 565800
FAX: (01483) 565807
E-MAIL: sales@fibrecrafts.co.uk
www.georgeweil.co.uk
*dyestuffs (synthetic and
natural), dyeing auxiliaries, fabric
paints, dyeing vessels and utensils,
screen-printing and batik
equipment, textile books*

Whaleys (Bradford) Ltd
Harris Court
Great Horton
Bradford BD7 4EQ
TEL: (01274) 576718
FAX: (01274) 521309
E-MAIL: whaleys@btinternet.com
www.whaleys-bradford.ltd.uk
*huge range of fabrics prepared for
dyeing and printing, including pre-
treated cloth for digital printing and
coated fabrics for ink jet printers;
minimum order £15*

Wolfin Textiles Ltd
359 Uxbridge Road
Hatch End
Middlesex HA5 4JN
TEL: (020) 8428 9911
FAX: (020) 8428 9955
CONTACT: Howard Wolfin
E-MAIL:
cotton@wolfintextiles.co.uk
www.wolfintextiles.co.uk
*basic cotton and linen fabrics,
including cotton duck for backing
cloths; very helpful service*

Wood and Wool
Withymoor Cottage
Burleydam, Whitchurch
Shropshire SY13 4BQ
TEL: (01948) 871618
CONTACT: Fiona Nisbet
E-MAIL: fionanisbet@yahoo.co.uk
*range of dyes and dyeing equipment
including syringes, thermometers,
litmus paper etc.*

UK Organisations

AN Magazine (formerly Artists'
Newsletter)
1st Floor, Turner Building
7–15 Pink Lane
Newcastle-upon-Tyne
NE1 5DW
TEL: (0191) 241 8000
FAX: (0191) 241 8001
information line: (0191) 241 8000
(daily 9.30am–6pm)
E-MAIL: info@anpubs.demon.co.uk
www.anweb.co.uk

Crafts Council
44A Pentonville Road
Islington, London N1 9BY
TEL: (020) 278 7700
E-MAIL: craft@craftscouncil .org.uk
www.craftscouncil.org.uk
OPEN: Tuesday–Saturday
11am–6pm / Sunday 2pm–6pm /
closed Monday

62 Group of Textile Artists
PO Box 24615
London E2 7TU
www.62group.freeuk.com

Society of Dyers & Colourists
PO Box 244, Perkin House
82 Grafton Road
Bradford BD1 2JB
TEL: (01274) 725138
FAX: (01274) 392888
E-MAIL: sales@sdc.org.uk
www.sdc.org.uk
The Colour Index

UK Galleries / Museums

Contemporary Applied Arts
2 Percy Street
London W1P 9FA
TEL: (020) 7436 2344
www.caa.org.uk
OPEN: Monday to Saturday
10.30am–5.30pm

Crafts Study Centre
The Surrey Institute of Art and
Design
University College
Falkner Road
Farnham
Surrey GU9 7DS
TEL/FAX: (01252) 719550

Museum of Costume
The Assembly Rooms
Bennett Street
Bath BA1 2QH
TEL: (01225) 477789
www.thecostumemuseum.co.uk
OPEN: Monday to Sunday
10am–5pm

The Burrell Collection
Glasgow Museums
2060 Pollockshaws Country Park
Glasgow G43 1AT
TEL: (main): (0141) 287 2550 / (textile conservator): (0141) 287 2566
OPEN: Monday to Thursday and
Saturday 10am–5pm
Friday and Sunday 11am–5pm

The Whitworth Art Gallery
University of Manchester
Oxford Road
Manchester M15 6ER
TEL: (0161) 275 7450
www.whitworth@man.ac.uk
OPEN: Monday to Saturday
10am–5pm, Sunday 2pm–5pm

Victoria & Albert Museum
Cromwell Road
London SW7 2RL
TEL: (020) 7942 2000
www.vam.ac.uk
OPEN: seven days 10am–5.45pm,
except Wednesdays 10am–10pm

USA
Suppliers

Aljo Manufacturing Co. Inc. Colors
81–83 Franklin Street
New York, NY 10013
TEL: 212–226–2878
large range of synthetic dyestuffs

Bayer Textile Chemicals
100 Bayer Road,
Pittsburgh
PA 15205–9741
TEL: 412–777–2000
www.bayertextile.com
pigments and auxiliaries

Calgon Corporation
PO Box 1346
Pittsburgh
PA 15230
TEL: 732–382–8982
FAX: 732–382–9326
www.inkmakeronline.com
pigments, colours, compounds

Calumet
branches across the US
New York, NY
TEL: 212–989–8500
FAX: 212–627–9088
archival quality photographic storage sheets (eg. for slides and 6″ x 4″ photo sheets for fabric samples)

Ciba Specialty Chemicals
N. America
560 White Plains Road
Tarrytown
NY 10591
TEL: 914–785–2000
www.cibasc.com/unitedstates
dyes and auxiliaries

Colorado Wholesale Dye
Corporation
5325 S. Broadway
Littleton
CO 80121
TOLL-FREE: 800–697–1566
TEL: 303–763–8774
www.bestdye.com
dyes and auxiliaries

Createx Colors
14 Airport Park Road
East Granby
CT 06026
TOLL-FREE: 800–243–2712
TOLL-FREE: 860–653–5505
(international orders)
FAX: 860–653–0643
www.createxcolours.com
range of dyes and pigments

DEKA Decart Inc.
PO Box 309
Morrisville
VT 05661
TEL: 802–888–4217
fabric paints

Dharma Trading Co.
PO Box 150916
San Rafael
CA 94915
TEL: 415-456-7657
TOLL-FREE: 800–542–5227
FAX: 415–456–8747
E-MAIL:
catalog@dharmatrading.com
www.dharmatrading.com
wide range of dyes and auxiliaries, fabric paints, transfer paper, batik equipment, brushes, fabrics, masks

Jacquard Products
Rupert, Gibbon & Spider, Inc.
PO Box 425
Healdsburg
CA 95448
TEL: 707–433–9577
TOLL-FREE: 800–442–0455
FAX: 707–433–4906
E-MAIL: jacquard@sonic.net
www.jacquardproducts.com
wide range of fabrics incl. ready-made scarves, silk painting and batik equipment, fabric paints, dyes and auxiliaries, stove-top and vertical steamers

Janlynn Corporation
34 Front Street
PO Box 51848
Indian Orchard
MA 01151–5848
TOLL-FREE: 800–445–5565
TEL: 413–543–7500
FAX: 413–543–7505
www.janlynn.com
wide range of dye supplies

Ohaus World Headquarters
PO Box 900,
19A Chapin Road
Pine Brook
NJ 07058
TEL: 973–377–9000
FAX: 973–593–0359
E-MAIL: OhausHW@Ohaus.com
precision scales (incl. triple beam balance)

PRO Chemical & Dye
PO Box 14
Somerset
MA 02777
TEL: 508–676–3838
(technical support & enquiries)
FAX: 508–676–3980
E-MAIL:
prochemical@worldnet.att.net
www.prochemical.com
wide range of dyes and auxiliaries, fabric paints, batik equipment, basic fabrics, books, colour matching service, lectures and workshops, technical information

Sericol Inc.
1101 West Cambridge Drive
Kansas City
KS 66103–1311
TOLL-FREE: 800–255–4562 (orders)
TEL: 913–342–4060
FAX: 913–342–4761
E-MAIL: sericoline@burma
castrol.com
www.sericol.com
wide range of screen-printing supplies

Testfabrics, Inc.
PO Box 26
West Pittston
PA 18643
TEL: 570–603–0432
FAX: 570–603–0433
CONTACT: Tom Klaas, Technical
Director
E-MAIL: testfabric@aol.com
www.testfabrics.com
wide range of fabrics prepared for printing, also fastness testing service

Thai Silks
252 State Street
Los Altos
CA 94022
TOLL-FREE: 800–221–7455
TEL: 650–948–8611
FAX: 650–948–3426
E-MAIL: info@thaisilks.com
www.thaisilks.com
distributors of natural silk by the yard

Ulano
255 Butler Street
Brooklyn
New York, NY 11217
TEL: 718–622–5200
FAX: 718–802–1119
photographic emulsion

USA Organisations

American Association of Textile
Chemists & Colorists
PO Box 12215
Research Triangle Park
NC 27709
TEL: 919–549–8141
FAX: 919–549–8933
E-MAIL: info@aatcc.org
www.aatcc.org

American Craft Council
72 Spring Street
New York
NY 10012–4019
TEL: 212–274–0630
FAX: 212–274–0650
www.craftcouncil.org

Arts, Crafts and Theater Safety
(ACTS)
181 Thompson Street # 23
New York, NY 10012–2586
TEL: 212–777–0062
E-MAIL: ACTSNYC@cs.com
www.caseweb.com/ACTS

Surface Design Association
PO Box 360
Sebastopol
CA 95473–0360
TEL: 707–829–3110
FAX: 707–829–3285
www.surfacedesign.org
membership: contact Joy
Stocksdale, Administrator
there is a quarterly newsletter as
well as the Surface Design Journal
(see publications)

Textile Society of America
PO Box 70
Earleville
MD 21919–0070
TEL: 410–275–2329
FAX: 410–275–8936
E-MAIL: tsa@dol.net
www.textilesociety.org

The Center for Safety in the Arts
www.artsnet.heinz.cmu.edu:70/1/c
sa

USA Galleries / Museums

American Crafts Museum
40 West 53rd Street
New York, NY 10019
TEL: 212–956–3535
www.americancraftmuseum.org

The Textile Museum
2320 South Street, NW
Washington DC
20008–4088
TEL: 202–667–0441
FAX: 202–483–0994
www.textilemuseum.org

CANADA
Suppliers

G & S Dye and Accessories Ltd
250 Dundas Street W.
Unit # 8
Toronto
Ontario M5T 2Z5
Canada
TEL: 416–596–0550
TOLL-FREE ORDERING: 800–596–0550
FAX: 416–596–0493
E-MAIL: sales@gsdye.com
www.gsdye.com
natural fabrics, silk scarves and ties, reactive, acid and silk painting dyes, fabric paint and pigments, chemicals, screen-printing equipment and services including screen reclamation, coating and exposing, printing, steaming, workshops and demos.

AUSTRALIA
Suppliers

Batik Oetoro
203 Avoca Street
Randwick, NSW 2031
TEL: 02–9398–6201
FAX: 02–9309–1173
E-MAIL: batikoetoro@one.net.au
www.web.one.net.au/batikoetoro
dyes, auxiliaries, related equipment including precision scales

Bayer Australia Ltd
PO Box 903
875 Pacific Highway
Pymble, NSW
TEL: 02–9391–6000
FAX: 02–9988–3311
www.bayer.com.au
pigments and auxiliaries

Calico House Homewares Pty Ltd
521 Chapel Street, South Yarra
VIC. 3141
(also has shops in Melbourne and Brisbane)
TEL: 03–9826–9957
FAX: 03–9827–2613
E-MAIL: calicohouse@pacific.net.au
cotton fabrics

Ciba Specialty Chemicals Pty Ltd
235 Settlement Road
Thomastown, VIC. 3074
TEL: 03–92–820–600
FAX: 03–94–659–070
www.cibasc.com/australia
dyes and auxiliaries

Colourmaker Industries Pty Ltd
44 Orchard Road
Brookvale, NSW 2100
TEL: 02–9939–7977
FAX: 02–9939–6685
pigments and specialist binders

Crode Australia
PO Box 6585
Wetherill Park, NSW 6124
TEL: 02–9756–4400
FAX: 02–9756–4414
www.croda.com
textile auxiliaries and printing inks

Elsegood Fabrics
R G Elsegood (Sales) Pty Ltd
Silk House
8 Little Queen Street
Chippendale, Sydney
NSW 2008
TEL: 02–9319–2266
FAX: 02–9699–8892
www.elsegood.com.au
silk specialist, wide range of fabrics prepared for printing, silk scarves, also dyed fabrics

Kraft Kolour Pty Ltd
Factory 11
242 High Street
Northcote, VIC. 3070
TEL: 03–9482–9234
FAX: 03–9482–9279
E-MAIL: kkolour@vegas.com.au
range of fabrics, scarves, dyes and auxiliaries, brushes, stencil and masking film, emulsion, screen mesh, screens and squeegees

Marie France
92 Currie Street
Adelaide, SA 5000
TEL/FAX: 08–8231–4138
E-MAIL:
mariefrance@adelaide.on.net
range of silks and silk paints, dyes and fabric paints, steamers; also runs a steaming service

Ohaus Australia
Unit 2/145 Faunce Street
Gosford, NSW 2250
TEL: 02–4322–2080
FAX: 02–4322–2082
E-MAIL: australiaSales@Ohaus.com
wide range of precision scales

Sericol Australia Pty Ltd
PO Box 6800
Kings Park, NSW 2148
TEL: 02–88–252–700
FAX: 02–96–218–100
www.
sericol.co.uk/XAustralia
wide range of screen-printing supplies, including drafting film (Seritrace)

Australia
Organisations

Craft Australia (the national organisation for professional craft)
Level 5
414–418 Elizabeth Street
Surry Hills, NSW 2010
TEL: 02–9211–1445
FAX: 02–9211–1443
E-MAIL: craft@craftaus.com.au
www.craftaus.com.au

Crafts Council of Australia
Directory of Archives in Australia
www.asap.unimelb.edu.au

NEW ZEALAND

Organisations

Creative New Zealand
Arts Council of New Zealand
Toi Aotearoa
PO Box 3806, Wellington
TEL: 04–498–0737
FAX: 04–473–0329
www.creativenz.govt.nz

PUBLICATIONS (UK, EUROPE AND USA)

American Craft (bi-monthly)
published by the American Crafts
Council
address as before

AN Magazine (monthly)
address as before
subscriptions TEL: (0191) 241 8000
FAX: (0191) 241 8001

Crafts (bi-monthly)
published by the Crafts Council
address as before
subscriptions TEL: (020) 7806 2542

Elle Decoration (monthly)
Endeavour House
189 Shaftesbury Avenue
London WC2H 8JG
subscriptions TEL: (01858) 438869
www.ukmagazines.co.uk

International Textiles (bi-monthly)
23 Bloomsbury Square
London WC1A 2PJ
TEL: (020) 7637 2211
FAX: (020) 7637 2248

Fiberarts (bi-monthly, but not
July/August)
50 College Street
Asheville
North Carolina 28801
TEL: 828–253–0467
FAX: 828–253–7952
E-MAIL: subscriptions@fiberarts-magazine.com

Surface Design Journal (quarterly)
(see also Surface Design
Association)
TEL: 707–829–3110
FAX: 707–829–3285
www.surfacedesign.org

Telos Art Publishing
(books: 'Art Textiles', 'Portfolio'
and 'Reinventing Textiles' series)
PO Box 125
Winchester
Hampshire SO23 7UJ
FAX: (01962) 864727
E-MAIL: sales@telos.net
www.arttextiles.com

Textile Forum (quarterly)
Textile Forum Service
PO Box 5944, D–30059
Hannover
Germany
TEL: 511–817–007
FAX: 511–813–108
E-MAIL: tfs@etn-net.org
www.etn-net.org

World of Interiors
Vogue House
Hanover Square
London W1S 1JU
subscriptions TEL: (01858) 438815 /
FAX: (01858) 461739
www.worldofinteriors.co.uk
www.thedesignstudio.com

BIBLIOGRAPHY

Broughton, Kate, *Textile Dyeing* Rockport Publishers Inc., Gloucester, Mass., USA, 1996

Clarke, W., *An Introduction to Textile Printing*, Butterworths in association with ICI Dyestuffs Division London, 1964, Third Edition 1971

Colchester, Chloë, *The New Textiles*, Thames & Hudson Ltd, London, 1991

Dryden, Deborah M., *Fabric Painting and Dyeing for the Theatre*, Heinemann Portsmouth NH, USA, 1993

Hardingham, Martin, *The Illustrated Dictionary of Fabrics*, Cassell & Collier MacMillan Publishers Ltd, 1978

Kendall, Tracy, *The Fabric & Yarn Dyers Handbook*, Collins & Brown, London, 2001

Koumis, Matthew, Ed., *Art Textiles of the World*: (series includes Great Britain Volumes 1 and 2, USA, Australia, Japan Volumes 1 and 2, The Netherlands, Scandinavia), Telos

Levi, Peta, Ed., *New British Design 1998*, Mitchell Beazley, London, 1998

McNamara, Andrea & Snelling, Patrick, *Design and Practice for Printed Textiles*, Oxford University Press South Melbourne, 1995

Milner, Ann, *The Ashford Book of Dyeing*, B T Batsford Ltd London, 1992

Ponting, K. G., *A Dictionary of Dyes and Dyeing*, Mills & Boon Ltd, London, 1980

Sterling Benjamin, Betsy, *The World of Rozome, Wax Resist Textiles of Japan*, Kodansha International Ltd, Tokyo, New York, London, 1996

Storey, Joyce, *The Thames and Hudson Manual of Dyes and Fabrics*, Thames and Hudson Ltd, London, 1978 (reprinted 1992)

Storey, Joyce, *The Thames and Hudson Manual of Textile Printing*, Thames and Hudson Ltd, London, 1974 (reprinted 1992)

Tompson, Frances and Tony, *Synthetic Dyeing*, David & Charles Publishers plc, Devon, 1987

Wellejus, Grethe, *Shibori Resist and Dyeing Techniques*, The Publishing House, Tomeliden, Denmark, 1989

Wells, Kate, *Fabric Dyeing and Printing*, Conran Octopus, London, 1997

INDEX OF ARTISTS

INDEX